The TURNING POINT for the U.K. and IRAN

SPIRITUAL INTERVIEWS WITH THE GUARDIAN SPIRITS OF JOHNSON, ROUHANI, KHAMENEI AND TRUMP

RYUHO OKAWA

HS PRESS

Contents

Preface 11

1

Spiritual Interview with
The Guardian Spirit of
Prime Minister Boris Johnson

2

Spiritual Interview with
The Guardian Spirit of President Rouhani

3

Spiritual Interview with
The Guardian Spirit of Ayatollah Khamenei

4

Spiritual Interview with
The Guardian Spirit of President Trump

5

Spiritual Messages from
The Guardian Spirit of Prime Minister Abe,
The Guardian Spirit of Greta Thunberg,
And Gaia

3   The Present and the Future Seen through the Eyes of
    Gaia

The following sections were originally recorded in Japanese and later translated
into English:

-Chapters 2 and 3, in full;
-Chapter 4, opening and closing comments;
-Chapter 5, Spiritual Messages from the Guardian Spirit of Prime Minister
Abe and Gaia, in full; interviewer's questions in Spiritual Messages from the
Guardian Spirit of Greta Thunberg, in part.

Preface

On December 17, 2019, the El Cantare Celebration was held at Saitama Super Arena in Japan. It was broadcasted live to 3,500 locations around the world, and the main event was to deliver my lecture ("To the Age of New Prosperity"). Just a few days before it, I thought I should do spiritual interviews with the world leaders' guardian spirits about the ongoing topics of international affairs, and find out the conclusions. This book is the report of the spiritual investigations.

The world leaders indeed have their problems. To find out their real thoughts is a premise to making the correct judgment.

Who is British Prime Minister Johnson, who won a landslide victory in the U.K. general election? What are the real thoughts of Iranian President Rouhani and top leader Khamenei? What does American President Trump think about the EU,

Hong Kong problem, and Iran problem? This book will reveal specific details I could not mention in the lecture.

Ryuho Okawa
Master & CEO of Happy Science Group
Dec. 23, 2019

1

Spiritual Interview with The Guardian Spirit of Prime Minister Boris Johnson

Recorded December 14, 2019
Special Lecture Hall, Happy Science, Japan

Boris Johnson (1964 - Present)

A British politician. A member of the British House of Commons, the leader of the Conservative Party, and the 77th prime minister. After graduating from the University of Oxford, Johnson worked as a conservative journalist and harshly criticized the idea of integrating Europe. He became a prominent figure of euroskepticism, and eventually led the Brexit movement in the 2016 EU referendum. Johnson served as the mayor of London and the foreign secretary before serving his current position, which he was appointed to in July 2019. In the 2019 U.K. general election, he said Brexit will be done by January 31, 2020 and led the Conservative Party to a landslide victory. His works include *The Churchill Factor*, and more.

Interviewers from Happy Science[*]

Motohisa Fujii
Executive Director
Special Assistant to Religious Affairs Headquarters
Director General of International Politics Division

Toshimitsu Yoshii
General Manager of International Politics Division
Religious Affairs Headquarters

No statements made by the guardian spirit of Mr. Boris Johnson in this book reflect statements actually made by Mr. Boris Johnson himself.

The opinions of the spirit do not necessarily reflect those of Happy Science Group. For the mechanism behind spiritual messages, see end section.

---

[*] Interviewers are listed in the order that they appear in the transcript. Their professional titles represent their positions at the time of the interview.

1

"The U.K.'s Trump" Confidently Claims Himself So

"I will be more than Thatcher and Churchill"

RYUHO OKAWA

Today, we have two issues. One is Boris Johnson's landslide, great victory in the U.K. It was yesterday. And, the next issue is the Iranian problem. Mr. President Rouhani of Iran will soon come to Japan and have a session with Prime Minister Abe. So, these are two topics.

And, in addition to that, Mr. Fujii translated and published *Trumponomics*,* it's a difficult English book. Mr. Fujii published this book at this El Cantare Festival.† It's very easy to understand

---

* Originally coauthored by Stephen Moore and Arthur B. Laffer.

† One of the two grand festivals of Happy Science that is held every December.

political issue and economic issue. Please read this *Trumponomics* in Japanese, and you can understand how our political opinion is correct. It's an additional one, just the propaganda.

Then, first one, about Boris Johnson's victory, and we want to know about his opinion regarding Japanese problem and around the world.

OK. I will [*claps once*] call him first.

Mr. Boris Johnson's guardian spirit,

Would you come down here?

This is Happy Science Japan.

Mr. Boris Johnson's guardian spirit,

Would you come down here?

[*About seven seconds of silence.*]

BORIS JOHNSON'S GUARDIAN SPIRIT
[*Laughs.*]

FUJII
Hello, good morning.

JOHNSON'S G.S.

Ah.

FUJII

Prime Minister Boris Johnson. Thank you for coming...

JOHNSON'S G.S.

Victory!

FUJII

...today, to Happy Science.

JOHNSON'S G.S.

Victory, victory, victory.

FUJII

Yes. You got a huge victory in the election.

JOHNSON'S G.S.

Yeah.

FUJII

What are you thinking now?

JOHNSON'S G.S.

Happy.

FUJII

Happy. Yes. You finally won.

JOHNSON'S G.S.

Brexit will be completed in the near future. [*Laughs.*]
Final decision-maker!

FUJII

You got a huge victory since Margaret Thatcher in
1987, so you're going to be a great prime minister.

JOHNSON'S G.S.

Great prime minister? OK. No problem.

FUJII

How are you going to make Britain?

JOHNSON'S G.S.

Greater than it used to be. I will be more than the great Margaret Thatcher and Winston Churchill.

Why he seeks for Brexit

FUJII

I think you're known as a euroskeptic figure. What is your opinion on the European Union? Why do you seek for Brexit?

JOHNSON'S G.S.

They are indecisive. They cannot make a decision. Just the animals talking! We have so much pride in the history of the United Kingdom. We must be and will be greater. We must protect our great history of victory. I'll be the U.K.'s Donald Trump, so all will be decided. It's OK, everything will be solved by me. So, no problem. No Europe. Only Boris Johnson's opinion will lead Europe.

FUJII
You talked about President Donald Trump. He was very supportive of you.

JOHNSON'S G.S.
Yeah.

FUJII
How do you see President Trump of the United States? You're very good friends.

JOHNSON'S G.S.
Yeah. Indeed. He's a nice guy, yeah.

FUJII

Do you agree with his opinion?

JOHNSON'S G.S.

And, a great leader, yeah, indeed. He is a man the world has been waiting for. And, I'm also the man... the savior of the U.K., of course.

FUJII

Today, actually, we don't have much time.

JOHNSON'S G.S.

Oh, really?

FUJII

So, I'll ask you very simple questions.

JOHNSON'S G.S.

Oh, I need two or three hours.

The Hong Kong issue
"Depends on Beijing"

FUJII

We want to ask very simple questions. Now, people in the world are concerned about the Hong Kong issue.

JOHNSON'S G.S.

Hong Kong issue?

FUJII

Hong Kong belonged to Great Britain for a long time. How do you see this situation?

JOHNSON'S G.S.

Ah, it depends on Beijing. If they give us a great chance for recovering in the economic meaning, I'll just say to protect human rights, but if Beijing will give us a little present for my victory, we will condemn them, "They are intruders or Hitler-like government." Yeah.

FUJII

How do you see Xi Jinping of China?

JOHNSON'S G.S.

I don't know. I don't know.

FUJII

You don't know?

JOHNSON'S G.S.

But they have money now. Please give us.

YOSHII

So, your plan is, you'll make Britain prosper with the help from China, you mean?

JOHNSON'S G.S.

It's one option, of course. The U.K. and the United States will make a great relationship, but we need another partner, of course. Between the EU and the

U.K., we have some wall in the meaning of trading, so we need another partner. China is one choice, and Japan or another country. Its design is just up to me.

FUJII

How do you see Japan? I think the relationship with Japan is very important for the U.K., but you might choose...

JOHNSON'S G.S.

If you introduce me in a great meaning, good meaning, I'll love you so much.

FUJII

You haven't made up your mind yet?

JOHNSON'S G.S.

But if you criticize me, "Boris Johnson is a small guy" or like that, I won't like you. I think Mr. Abe is at the situation of his last day. I think so. So, I want to know the next strategy of Japan. He cannot decide anything. I guess so.

2

Spiritual Connection with Churchill and Thatcher

Experience as a Japanese and a Chinese
In his past lives

FUJII

I have great respect in you. You wrote a book about Winston Churchill.

JOHNSON'S G.S.

Yes. Yeah.

FUJII

So, I think you have a close connection with Churchill in the Spirit World.

JOHNSON'S G.S.

Yes. Of course. Of course.

FUJII

What kind of connection do you have with him? Is he guiding you?

JOHNSON'S G.S.

Winston Churchill sometimes came to me and said, "I have a great connection with Ryuho Okawa of Happy Science." He said so. I don't know exactly, it's a religious relationship? But yeah, he said, "Mr. Okawa in Japan is reliable," so yeah. I have much concern about you.

FUJII

When you visited us last time for just a short time, you talked not in English, but in Japanese.

JOHNSON'S G.S.
Oh.

FUJII

I suppose you can speak it.

JOHNSON'S G.S.

Was that Japanese?

FUJII

A little bit.

JOHNSON'S G.S.

Oh. I want to talk...

FUJII

Did you happen to be a Japanese in your past life? Or, do you have much interest in Japanese history or so?

JOHNSON'S G.S.

Oh. My past life?

FUJII

Yes. Do you like Japan?

JOHNSON'S G.S.

Hmm... I might be the reincarnation of Confucius.

FUJII

Uh, I'm not sure [*laughs*].

JOHNSON'S G.S.

You cannot believe me? Then, then, then, the next step is a disciple of Confucius.

FUJII

OK [*laughs*]. So, you mean you were born in China, not in Japan.

JOHNSON'S G.S.

Ah, in China and Japan, of course. I have an experience.

Of course, I can speak Japanese. But the listeners are the problem. Japanese people only, or foreign people?

FUJII

I suppose both of them.

"Thatcher and Churchill gave me power"

YOSHII

From another aspect of spiritual connection, Margaret Thatcher highly evaluated your article. Firstly, as a journalist, you wrote an article about euroskepticism. As a euroskeptic journalist, you were a front-runner. So, do you have a spiritual connection with Margaret Thatcher?

JOHNSON'S G.S.

Hmm. Yeah, we have many conferences in the heavenly world, yeah. She is one of the guiding spirits, yeah. Margaret Thatcher and Winston Churchill. And, they gave me every power on how to decide and lead the U.K. All are in my hand.

So, the EU is a weaker countries' gathering, it's just so. We must be one country, and a great country. The U.K. should be the leader of the world. So, we need Brexit. Thatcher agreed about that. Winston Churchill, also. Winston Churchill said that France and Germany cannot be relied on, and was also skeptical about their goodwill. So, we need economic growth and the political leadership for the world. It's also a Japanese problem. I think so.

But the relationship with the U.K. and Japan, Japan and the United States, and the United States and the U.K., this triangle will be very happy, and will be successful in the making of the future of the world.

3

His Stance On China and The Middle East, and More

To China:
"Just make investments in our country"

FUJII

This might be the last question. I believe you are the very key person to change the world. You mentioned China and Xi Jinping, but I'll ask you more on that. What do you think of communism?

JOHNSON'S G.S.

I don't like communism, but I have the sympathy for weaker people, of course. In that meaning, I have some intention to save weaker people; it's not just "give something to them," but "make themselves be independent and by themselves, for themselves," and the next Industrial Revolution will occur from the U.K., I think.

You asked me about Hong Kong? If Hong Kong people help us, we will make rearrangement between Hong Kong and the U.K. Yeah, of course. They can be one of the groups of Great Britain in the world, like Australia, Canada, India, or so. I will make Great Britain's world strategy again, yeah.

FUJII

OK. Another question is about "One Belt, One Road" strategy. Xi Jinping is invading Europe by his economic strategy.

JOHNSON'S G.S.

It's OK. If possible, it's OK. Please invest in our country and never ask for our return. Just make investments. It's OK. But we don't have the same opinion in the political meaning, economic meaning, and world diplomacy.

I will be keeping in touch with Mr. Donald Trump, and the world strategy regarding political and foreign, diplomatic meaning, we are the same with the United States. So, we will, I will welcome the great investment from China, but in the political meaning, we don't agree with Xi Jinping.

FUJII
OK. I understand.

YOSHII
You mentioned the next Industrial Revolution.

JOHNSON'S G.S.
Yeah.

YOSHII
So, what kind of technology are you focusing on?

JOHNSON'S G.S.

I don't know exactly. So, it's my hope. I'm a prime minister, so I just make a decision and should indicate the direction of our country. "We'll be great again, greater again," I will repeat like Donald Trump. So, it will open a new way for the new start entrepreneurs. We will help them, and there will follow a lot of geniuses from the U.K., and we will gather such kind of great people from all over the world.

About the Middle East problem, "We will choose the same direction As Trump"

FUJII

OK. Thank you for your message. It's high time to conclude.

JOHNSON'S G.S.
Oh, really? Tomorrow, again!

FUJII
Do you have another message?

JOHNSON'S G.S.
Another message.

FUJII
Is it OK to conclude your message today?

JOHNSON'S G.S.
[*To the audience.*] Is there any additional question for me? Do you love me? I'm very kind to ladies. Hmm. No?

FUJII
How do you see the Middle East problem? Iranian issue is very critical just now.

JOHNSON'S G.S.

Ah, yeah, hmm. It's complicated, but we will make a safeguard to our transportation from the Middle East area to the U.K., in the meaning of oil import. So, we'll have a new conversation with Donald Trump and make a decision about the Iranian problem or other problems of the Middle East, for example, Syria or Israel or Saudi Arabia or other problems. Yeah, yeah.

The main leader is now, Mr. Donald Trump. We will choose the same direction, but at this time, I cannot tell what is correct, I mean, if the Iranian leaders are evil or not. I'm not sure in this point today.

FUJII

Thank you for your message today.

JOHNSON'S G.S.

OK. Ah, very short.

FUJII

Just for a short time.

JOHNSON'S G.S.

Previous time, only 10 minutes. Today, only 25 minutes.

FUJII

No, 30 minutes.

JOHNSON'S G.S.

This is your respect for the...

FUJII

We respect you very much.

JOHNSON'S G.S.

...prime minister of the United Kingdom? We are the lost world or...

FUJII

The U.K. is a very important country.

JOHNSON'S G.S.

Really?

FUJII

Yes, we believe so.

JOHNSON'S G.S.

Hmm. Please come to the U.K.

FUJII

Yes, of course.

JOHNSON'S G.S.

Ah, [*laughs*] we have no good British dish, nothing, [*clicks tongue*] like for example, the Japanese dishes, or French or Turkish or Chinese-like delicious dishes. Just eat beef or fish and enjoy it.

FUJII

OK. We hope to see you again next time. Thank you so much for today.

JOHNSON'S G.S.

You are planning to come to...

FUJII

Yes, London in Britain. Next year (2020).

JOHNSON'S G.S.

Ah, hmm, yeah.

FUJII

We hope to see you soon.

JOHNSON'S G.S.

It's hopeful and helpful. We need Japanese great connection, and I'm waiting for you.

FUJII

OK, thank you so much.

JOHNSON'S G.S.

It's not enough, but... I'll say goodbye.

FUJII

[*Laughs.*] We look forward to the next time. Thank you so much. Goodbye.

RYUHO OKAWA

Then, next, the Iranian problem. We already know about them, and they can easily speak Japanese. How should I deal with them?

FUJII

Japanese is better.

RYUHO OKAWA

Japanese is better? OK then, Hassan Rouhani, first.

2

Spiritual Interview with The Guardian Spirit of President Rouhani

Recorded December 14, 2019
Special Lecture Hall, Happy Science, Japan

Hassan Rouhani (1948 - Present)

An Iranian politician. A cleric of Shia Islam. After graduating from the University of Tehran, he studied at Glasgow Caledonian University in the U.K. and earned a PhD. He returned to Iran after the Iranian Revolution and participated in the Iran-Iraq War, serving as a member of the High Council for National Defense, commander of Iran Air Defense Force, and deputy commander of the war. He was known as an advisor to the moderate former President Hashemi Rafsanjani, and was the chief nuclear negotiator of Iran from 2003 to 2005. In 2013, he became the president of Iran after winning the majority vote in the presidential election.

Interviewers from Happy Science

Same as Chapter 1.

1

President of Iran's Thinking Regarding His Visit to Japan

Summoning the guardian spirit of President Rouhani before his visit to Japan

RYUHO OKAWA

Iranian President Hassan Rouhani.

Iranian President Hassan Rouhani.

You will be coming to Japan soon.

Prime Minister Abe is very concerned,

And seems to be very worried

What he should do.

Imam Rouhani's guardian spirit,

Please come down to Happy Science

And tell us what is on your mind.

[*About 10 seconds of silence.*]

PRESIDENT ROUHANI'S GUARDIAN SPIRIT
Hmm... Troublesome.

FUJII
Are you President Rouhani?

ROUHANI'S G.S.
Yeah...

FUJII
Thank you very much.

ROUHANI'S G.S.
What should we do?

FUJII
OK. Iran is in a very difficult situation right now.

ROUHANI'S G.S.
We are in trouble, in great trouble...

FUJII

We don't have so much time today, so could you deliver a simple message or tell us what you are thinking?

ROUHANI'S G.S.

Umm, that's what I want to ask you. What can you guys do?

FUJII

Oh...

ROUHANI'S G.S.

What can you do now? Tell me.

FUJII

There is only so much that the Japanese government can do. But you can rely on Happy Science.

ROUHANI'S G.S.
Ah [*clicks tongue*]. Hmm, well... I will be coming to Japan.

FUJII
Yes.

ROUHANI'S G.S.
I'm thinking to basically make stronger the ties between the Islamic countries and also build a bond with Japan because it can be a bridge between us and the Christian nations, but I don't rely too much. It would be so much easier if you were a part of the ruling party, but it's difficult at this point, I guess. Mr. Abe... I think he can do nothing. Yeah.

Iran is suffering from oil sanctions

FUJII

The U.S.-Iran relations are quite tense right now, so I believe you are expecting Japan to be a mediator.

ROUHANI'S G.S.

Yesterday, the stock prices went up because the U.S. is thinking to shelve the trade war between China... I guess Boris's victory in the election influenced it, too. But I think that shelving the trade war with China means that they are thinking to attack Iran soon.

FUJII

I see. Yes, OK.

ROUHANI'S G.S.

Yeah. This is bad.

FUJII

Have you thought of any countermeasures...

ROUHANI'S G.S.

Umm, we want them to attack Beijing first, you know?

FUJII

I agree.

ROUHANI'S G.S.

Then, we will be postponed.

FUJII

Yes, OK.

ROUHANI'S G.S.

You know? Iran is in trouble right now. OK? Our oil doesn't sell, so we lost two-thirds of our merchandise. What are we going to do next year? Our people are angry.

FUJII

Uh huh.

ROUHANI'S G.S.

Yeah, they are holding demonstrations. I guess the Japanese people might not understand why they are demonstrating, but oil is very cheap in Iran. I think, in Japan, people pay about one or two dollars per liter, right?

FUJII

Yes, right.

ROUHANI'S G.S.

OK. In Iran, oil used to be about 10 cents. And, if the price rises to 20, 30 cents and more, it will be much harder for people to live because everyone drives a car. Also, we are starting to feel the effects of the sanctions. Meat, vegetables and things like that are soaring in price as a result of inflation, making it difficult for us to live. But the Hong

Kong demonstrations and the Iran demonstrations are different. The Hong Kong demonstrations occurred because of the violent oppression by the police. It's a human rights issue. In the case of Iran, it's a problem of struggle for survival and inflation.

FUJII
Yes.

ROUHANI'S G.S.
But this inflation is not caused by us. It occurred due to sanctions mainly by the U.S. We have to do something about this. Hmm [*clicks tongue*], I don't know what to do.

"Please buy oil"

FUJII
The Japanese government will talk with the U.S. before they meet with Iran's leader, President

Rouhani. Knowing that, what do you expect from the Japanese government? Could you just tell us today, what...

ROUHANI'S G.S.

You mean, sending Japan's Self-Defense Forces (JSDF)? Mr. Abe will want to get approval to send the self-defense forces, right? Maybe.

FUJII

Yes. I think so.

ROUHANI'S G.S.

What does he want to do by sending them? I don't know.

FUJII

You can ask Prime Minister Abe, but there are things he can do and he cannot do. What do you expect from him at this time? If you could clarify that in a message...

ROUHANI'S G.S.

Umm, please buy oil.

FUJII

OK.

ROUHANI'S G.S.

Please buy oil from us. Not just for one year, but please make a decision to buy for five years or ten years in the form of a contract. Then, the U.S.-led coalition of the willing cannot attack the oil facilities in Iran.

FUJII

Right.

ROUHANI'S G.S.

Yeah, so buy our oil. If he says so, then even if the JSDF comes to our neighborhood, they can say that they are protecting the oil being transported to Japan. It means Japan will not want the U.S. to attack Iran so much because the Japanese economy will be hit. If Iran can get money, the people can rest easy and live their future. If more sanctions are imposed than as it is, we will have no trading partners. Russia says they will lend us, but we can trade with only Russia, China, and North Korea. They are "countries of caution" for you. So, is that good for you?

FUJII
No, it's not.

ROUHANI'S G.S.
Japan would be in trouble. In any case, Japan will be in trouble. Mr. Abe will come to a dead end. So, if he makes Mr. Trump look good, then Xi Jinping will look bad, and if he makes Xi Jinping look good, then Mr. Trump and Rouhani will look bad. He will have to pay for trying to look good to everyone, so he will come to a dead end, for sure.

FUJII

OK.

Japan would be in trouble
If the Middle East were to be in flames

FUJII

We are planning to talk to the guardian spirit of Ayatollah Khamenei after this session.

ROUHANI'S G.S.

Ah, OK.

FUJII

Time is limited, so today, we would like to focus on hearing about your visit to Japan. In Japanese diplomacy, given the U.S.-Japan relationship, I don't think Mr. Abe can be supportive toward Iran. In light of what is about to happen in the future, is there anything that you want Japan to do?

ROUHANI'S G.S.

Japan is an independent nation, so even if there is the Japan-U.S. security treaty, Mr. Trump might say, "Give us more money for keeping the U.S. military bases there. If not, protect your own country by yourself." For him, the Japan-U.S. alliance is just a business deal. It could change anytime, anyhow. The U.S. can get their own oil, coal, and natural gas all on their own, so they don't care about the Islamic countries in the Middle East. Even if they were to be in flames, the U.S. has nothing to lose from that.

FUJII

Right.

ROUHANI'S G.S.

But Japan will be in trouble, I think. He (Mr. Trump) wants to reduce unemployment in his own country and raise wages. If the Middle East were to be in flames, the U.S. can produce more shale oil, shale gas, and coal, and create jobs. Then, their domestic economy will be a lot better. That is what he is thinking about. And, if the crude oil from the Middle East does not sufficiently reach Europe, China and Japan, then those countries will be in trouble, but it means the U.S. can take the initiative. Yeah.

FUJII

OK. We would like to invite the guardian spirit of Ayatollah Khamenei now. Do you have anything more to say?

ROUHANI'S G.S.

Hmm... He sent 14,000 more troops. He wants to put on a performance, so that he can be re-elected in the next presidential election. I think so. If it's a performance, hmm, it will be before the sandstorms, so... It's the same as the old Gulf

War, so we could be attacked suddenly, as early as January or February (2020). We will fight back, but it will be a waste if the oil for Japan burned up.

FUJII
Yes. I think so, too.

ROUHANI'S G.S.
Yeah. What a waste.

FUJII
Yes.

ROUHANI'S G.S.
Please buy oil, we will make it half the price. It would be a waste if it burns. And, think about all the CO_2 it will emit, you know, if they attack or make a war. So, you need to teach Mr. Abe the significance of Japan's mediation.

FUJII

OK.

2

Advice to Japan

"No coal" "no oil" "no nuclear" means Japan has no future

ROUHANI'S G.S.

Japan is in trouble now, right? People tell you, "no coal," "no oil," "no nuclear," so what are you going to do? You would have problems with wind and solar panel when a typhoon comes, right?

FUJII

Yes.

ROUHANI'S G.S.

You have no future. If you use coal, people get angry because it emits CO_2. And, Minister of the Environment Koizumi received a "Fossil of the Day" award. His father is against nuclear power.

FUJII

Yes.

ROUHANI'S G.S.

Japan has no future. What are you going to do? You cannot supply your own energy and you cannot provide your own food, either. It's easy to make Japan starve. If someone controls your energy and food, it's over for you. So, if the Chinese navy controls the Pacific sea lane or gets marine hegemony over the Pacific, your food will stop coming in. It's very much possible.

FUJII

Yes.

ROUHANI'S G.S.

You can transport by plane, but they have their air force, so they can shoot down your planes. Then, you will starve. Lack of oil and lack of food, both. Japan has a little coal, but it's not enough to support everyone. Wind and solar power only are not effective because Japan has small area of land. So, Japan has to make a decision now, or it will end.

FUJII
OK.

Prime Minister Abe must say "Japan First"

FUJII
So, you are saying that this is important for Japan to secure its own energy.

ROUHANI'S G.S.
Yeah. So, don't try to look good to the U.S., China, and the U.K. The Japanese prime minister must say it first before others talk about it. "Japan can only develop if it does this!" Japan first. Right now, Japan first. Mr. Abe must say "Japan First". It needs to be said.

FUJII

OK. Thank you for your precious message.

ROUHANI'S G.S.

After all, Russia is still unlikely to provide such a stable supply of natural gas, and no energy will come from China. China is already buying coal from Mongolia and other places. In the end, they might even attack and take the Middle East.

So, Iran, Iran... Saudi Arabia is the guilty one, no matter how you look at it. They have Mecca, the holy land for Islamic countries, but they have U.S. military bases there and are plotting with Israel. There is something wrong about this. Really, something wrong. Religiously, it's wrong.

FUJII

OK. We would also like to hear about the religious issues from Ayatollah Khamenei...

ROUHANI'S G.S.
Yeah, yeah. OK.

FUJII
Can we finish for today?

ROUHANI'S G.S.
Yeah.

FUJII
Thank you very much.

ROUHANI'S G.S.
It's a little disappointing... I'll come, but I'll have to go home empty-handed, maybe.

FUJII
I see.

ROUHANI'S G.S.
It's a little sad.

Japan must change
Into a religious nation soon

ROUHANI'S G.S.

[*Clicks tongue.*] Ah, you guys, can't you do more? If you can do a bit more... Can't you be the minister of economy, trade and industry? No? Like that.

FUJII

We have the Happiness Realization Party, so we will do our best.

ROUHANI'S G.S.

But in the elections... It is also said that, "Now, Japan is a nation that suppresses religions. In reality, it's like North Korea and China." So, you need to change it into a religious nation soon. You, a religious party, cannot get votes, right?

FUJII

Right.

ROUHANI'S G.S.

Because the mass media hinders you and keeps you from getting votes. I've heard that they don't even let you run commercials.

FUJII

That's right.

ROUHANI'S G.S.

Hmm. You are saying good things, but they don't praise you. Right? Japan would be much different if the mass media talked more about things like *Iran no Hanron* (lit. "Iran's Counterargument") [*Holds up* Nihon no Shimei (*lit. "The Mission of Japan"*) *and* Leader Kokka Nihon no Shinro (*lit. "The Course of Leader Nation Japan"*)]*. But they don't take you seriously, right? This comes from the wrong values of post-war Japan, so it should be corrected.

---

* All three books are Tokyo: IRH Press, 2019.

FUJII

OK.

ROUHANI'S G.S.

So, it's "Japan First". You should change it. Japan must say what it must. I want Japan to be a religious nation. Then, you can understand how Iran feels.

FUJII

Yes. OK. So, we have to be "Japan First". Thank you very much.

RYUHO OKAWA

OK [*claps three times*].

3

Spiritual Interview with The Guardian Spirit of Ayatollah Khamenei

Recorded December 14, 2019
Special Lecture Hall, Happy Science, Japan

Ali Khamenei (1939 - Present)

An Iranian religious figure and politician. After studying at a seminary in Najaf, one of the holy cities of Shia Islam, he went on to study at a seminary in Qom under Khomeini. Khamenei participated in the Iranian Revolution, and after that, served posts such as a member of the council of the Islamic Revolution, the deputy defense minister, the head of revolutionary guards, and the secretary of the supreme national security council. He was elected the president of Iran in 1981, and re-elected in 1985. In 1989, after the passing of Khomeini, the first supreme leader, Khamenei became the second supreme leader of Iran.

Interviewers from Happy Science

Same as Chapter 1.

1

Voicing Opinions
To Japan and the U.S.

Summoning the guardian spirit of
Ayatollah Khamenei, Iran's religious leader

FUJII

Then, please call Ayatollah Khamenei.

RYUHO OKAWA

Ayatollah Ali Khamenei, the religious leader above the president. Now, people are demonstrating [*claps softly*] saying, "Death to Khamenei." [*Rubs hands together.*] We have already received spiritual messages from Ayatollah Khamenei five times. Is there something you want to say? Anything to say?

AYATOLLAH KHAMENEI'S GUARDIAN SPIRIT

Hmm.

FUJII

Thank you for coming.

KHAMENEI'S G.S.

[*Clicks tongue.*]

FUJII

Are you Ayatollah Khamenei?

KHAMENEI'S G.S.

Umm.

FUJII

Again and again, we...

KHAMENEI'S G.S.

We are in trouble. You published some books [*holds up aforementioned* Nihon no Shimei *and other books*], but they are not selling that much. It might be so.

FUJII

The situation in Iran is becoming increasingly tense, and I believe that the Iranian regime is in danger.

KHAMENEI'S G.S.

Let's form a Japan-Iran alliance. Then, as long as we have oil, we will provide oil for Japan, permanently or semi-permanently. For example, I mean.

FUJII

Uh huh.

"I want President Trump To clear things with China first"

FUJII

Today, we have very little time left before the El Cantare Festival, so we hope to hear some short but important messages from you. Moments ago, we talked to the guardian spirit of President Rouhani about his visit to Japan, and he said, "Please buy oil," "Japan First," and "Become a religious nation." On the other hand, for Iran, I guess there are aspects that need to be reformed. What do you think about that?

KHAMENEI'S G.S.

Hmm, that's a little... I guess so. You know, it seems like Mr. Trump [*clicks tongue*] might stop halfway regarding China. El Cantare"'s thinking is to clear things up with China first, then reform Islam.

---

* The Supreme God of the Earth Spirit Group; God of the Earth who has guided humanity since the beginning of the Earth and who was also involved in the Creation of the universe. The core consciousness of El Cantare has descended as "Alpha" 330 million years ago, "Elohim" 150 million years ago, and Ryuho Okawa in Japan now. See Ryuho Okawa, *The Laws of the Sun: One Source, One Planet, One People* and *The Laws of Faith: One World Beyond Differences* (both New York: IRH Press, 2018).

FUJII

That's right. Yes.

KHAMENEI'S G.S.

But Mr. Trump is doing them at the same time, so he is always having trouble deciding which he should do first. Please clear up Hong Kong and Uyghur, also. I mean, they are in trouble, too.

FUJII

OK.

Iran is now driven into a corner, Just like Japan in WWII

KHAMENEI'S G.S.

You know, the demonstrations in Iran? It's been widely reported that people were killed, but a country cannot keep itself if its income falls to about one-third of now. I can understand that they are getting violent. They are not getting violent because it's a matter of good and evil, but because they cannot survive. It's the same as Japan. We are driven into a corner, just like the "ABCD encirclement" of Japan in WWII. Yeah, indeed. So, he is waiting to see if we will do something after he puts pressure on us. I'm sure he is trying to get Iran to make the first attack on U.K. and U.S. forces deployed to Saudi Arabia and the Middle East. That is why he is cornering us.

Inflation is going up higher, you know? We cannot last so much longer. But we didn't do anything to deserve this. And, Israel is now very questionable. Mr. Trump loves Netanyahu, but we don't even know if his own Israel people trust him or not. Or, maybe Mr. Trump wants to use Israel to control us. It seems so.

It might be to keep Russia in check, also. Russia is blocked by the EU, so they are trying to come out to the Middle East. It looks like the U.S. is trying to block Russia by increasing U.S. military hegemony in the Middle East.

FUJII
OK.

Ayatollah Khamenei sees through America's aim

FUJII
Now, you are likely in the eve of war, but what you are saying is that Iran doesn't want to fight, right?

KHAMENEI'S G.S.
We will lose if we go to war. Of course, we will. In conclusion, a lot of important resources on Earth will be lost. Hmm. [*Clicks tongue.*] Umm,

the price of oil could go up instead, bringing an "oil inflation" for oil importing countries. I don't know if they will shift to natural gas or coal after that. And, in conclusion, Japan will be made to buy expensive shale oil or coal or natural gas from the U.S. I think so. You will be approached like that. Mr. Trump thinks a lot about making money, so I think that is how it will be. Yeah.

FUJII

So, do you think this Iranian situation is highly likely to be disadvantageous for Japan?

KHAMENEI'S G.S.

The U.S. has about the same amount of coal in reserve as Saudi Arabia does with oil. The U.S. coal industry was doing very poor, but Mr. Trump is trying to revive it now. He is bringing back coal mining and trying to create more businesses around it. People are saying, "American coal will last for another 500 years." And, Japan is about to shift to coal now, so the U.S. will sell you their coal soon. If you join in the sanctions against Iran, you will be forced to buy a lot of American coal. They will say, "We will let you sell us some Japanese beef, so buy our coal." I guess so. And, I think they will try to prevent you from getting natural gas from Russia. The Middle East will be in flames soon.

So, umm... He wants Jewish-American votes for his re-election, I guess. I understand that. Many of them are right wing, so I can understand, but umm [*clicks tongue*], it doesn't sound so good.

Japan must find a way to survive

KHAMENEI'S G.S.
Japan must really find a way to survive, or you will be in danger. You can also buy coal from Australia, but the Asian waters will soon be under the control

of the Chinese forces, so this route is in danger, too. Weapons like the U.S. fighters and the Seventh Fleet can protect Japan, but if the U.S. and China make a deal, then soon, Japan cannot protect the goods coming in from overseas. So, you have to be careful.

Mr. Trump is a nice guy for Japan, I guess, but he makes deals. He will definitely choose the sweet side of the deal. If China offers a good deal, he will surely take that over Japan because he is a businessperson. He is trying to weaken the EU, also. He is trying to dissolve the EU by suggesting that the U.K. become independent, so that no country can compete with the U.S. He is doing this now.

Hmm, it's a... You know, the Islamic countries in the Middle East are divided into sects, so it might seem like we are not friends. But actually, we must not be so divided in the meaning of belief. So, umm... [*clicks tongue*] if he is going to attack the Islamic Middle East, then making Uyghur free from China is a dream within a dream.

In some meaning, Mr. Trump is a good person, I guess. He can do it for the U.S., but Japan needs to work harder to bring balance to parts of the world that lack it. In these past decades, the Chinese economy grew hundreds of times larger, but Japan only doubled or tripled. Something is wrong, you know? Japan really needs to become independent.

Many people in the Middle East like Japan. So, we would be glad if you let us supply oil to Japan, and if China's "One Belt, One Road" will obstruct Japan's sea lane, we will support Japan's increase in defense power. We want you to defend yourself properly, and I think you can protect the ports where Japanese tankers make stops from coming under the control of Chinese forces. But if China says they want to buy oil from us, then... We will be tempted a little, so it will be difficult to make a decision. I think Japan is in a very tough position right now.

2

Promoting the Legitimacy of Islam

Reforms are underway in Iran

FUJII

I'm really sorry. We are almost out of time.

KHAMENEI'S G.S.

Oh.

FUJII

Finally, I would like to ask where the Islamic reform is headed. According to "Spiritual Messages from God Thoth"[*] given recently during Master's missionary tour to Canada, it was revealed that the Islamic world was in need of reform. At present,

---

[*] Recorded on the day before the author's lecture in Canada, "The Reason We Are Here" (Oct. 6, 2019). See Chapter 4 in Ryuho Okawa, *The Reason We Are Here: Make Our Powers Together to Realize God's Justice - China Issue, Global Warming, and LGBT -* (Tokyo: HS Press, 2020).

there is a risk of war, but how are you perceiving the fact that the Islamic world need reforms from the perspective of world history?

KHAMENEI'S G.S.

After the Khomeini Revolution, it seemed like we were going back to Islamic fundamentalism, like reactionism. (Mr. Trump) might be thinking that we are going against the trend of westernization. To him, the Islamic Revolution is a bad thing, but he is trying to accept the China after the Mao Tse-tung Revolution. Just in terms of economy, they are working hard to make money.

I think we are seen as totalitarians, and umm... We are making some reform still now, but I guess it's slow. We are still expanding women's rights, you know? But it looks slow from their side, I guess. And, we do not have enough promotional strategy through the news in our world, so we will be in serious trouble unless we deepen our connection with some leading country, I think.

Destroying Iran will lead to Something quite serious

KHAMENEI'S G.S.

Anyway, to me, it seems that many countries will "prey" on Iran. Iraq, in the end, also was defeated on false charges, you know? Iraq was occupied for allegedly having weapons of mass destruction and chemical weapons, and the president was tried and killed. It was discovered that there were no weapons of mass destruction or chemical weapons, but still, people were killed and the country occupied. It was outrageous. And, there seem to be more guerrillas everywhere. They are in tough times. There are many problems like the Islamic State problem.

If they attack and destroy Iran, they will have to deal with more. People will go their own ways, and many guerrillas... The U.S. wants to prevent guerrilla activities and Islamic terrorism, and that is their assignment for this century, so they should not try to create more guerrillas. It's OK while we are in control. They might be thinking that Iran will become a democracy if they kill the top people like myself, but for Iran, democratizing it means almost the same as making it a country that doesn't believe in God. This will lead to something quite serious.

Iran values religious sentiment

KHAMENEI'S G.S.

The Communist Revolution started by Mao has been based on materialism and atheism, and El Cantare is saying that it's wrong, so it should be corrected. We don't have anything to show the relationship between Elohim*, Allah, and El Cantare yet, so we cannot say clearly, but I think

---

* One of the core consciousnesses of El Cantare, the Supreme God of the Earth Spirit Group. Elohim was born about 150 million years ago, near the area that is now the Middle East, and taught teachings of wisdom, mainly on the differences of light and darkness, and good and evil. Elohim is the same being as Allah in Islam. See aforementioned *The Laws of Faith*.

we (and Happy Science) have a common feeling to value religious sentiment.

You can support Israel, but it would not benefit you at all. Japan was defeated by atomic bombs that were made because of Einstein, who was Jewish, you know? And, Jewish people were made in Israel. I don't think there is any good reason you have to be on the side of the Jews. In fact, Japan should have the Jews apologize for that. The Pope visited Japan and said, "Do not fight a war," "Do not make an atomic bomb," "Do not promote nuclear power." He also said, "Do not buy coal from Europe" and "Do not use coal." Now, countries are trying to stop Japan from using oil, so it's not good. Japan needs to be more clear in its design.

We have a lot of small guerrillas, so I don't know them all, but at the least, I can say that Iran is not such kind of barbaric country that attacks Saudi Arabia, under the command of the supreme leader or the president, or that attacks Japanese ships and tankers while the Japanese prime minister is visiting us. I think we are being set up in the same trap as the one Iraq under Saddam Hussein experienced. The CIA and Mossad* are trying to lead us according to their scenario, but they will see the opposite result, I think. Soon, you will see that it was all set up by them.

If they wage a war, you will know the truth after it ends, so I hope they don't. I don't want them to make the same mistake again. We cannot convey this enough because we are poor at communicating. We are at a small disadvantage because of our language.

---

* The national intelligence agency of Israel formed in 1949. Its main responsibilities include intelligence collection and covert operations.

"I wish both Mr. Johnson and Mr. Trump Were Muslims"

KHAMENEI'S G.S.

But you know... Boris Johnson that you interviewed earlier? He has been married several times and had "first girlfriend" or "second girlfriend" or like that, right? He just needs to convert to Islam. You know? Then, he can have like four wives at the same time. He should not divorce every time and put a burden on his family. He is very energetic, so he can have four. Just convert to Islam. OK? So, we are right.

Look at what he is doing. The British prime minister is really Muslim, no matter how you look at it. So, we are not wrong. Because people say it's bad, it ends up on the front page of a weekly magazine and creates trouble. The world is getting more lenient now. Mr. Trump, also. If he were Muslim, he could have fought with the mass media over fake news more easily.

So, umm... [*Clicks tongue.*] I want them to understand us better, but there was that Iranian incident in the past. They make a movie about Americans escaping Iran and advertised how scary Iran is. I guess that memory is imprinted on everyone's mind, but we are very different from North Korea. Basically, we defend, but not invade.

Warning again
On the danger of attacking Iran

KHAMENEI'S G.S.

Attacking Iran following the attack on Iraq? If they really go as far as burning all of Iran's petroleum facilities, I think the Iranians who have scattered all over the world, including many in the U.S., will do something. I cannot stop this. I will already be killed at the time, I think. I cannot stop it. A religious leader like me can say, "Don't do it" and I think it would have some power to stop things like that, but Mr. Trump is thinking of killing us with a drone, I'm sure.

He can control a drone from within the U.S. and aim where Khamenei is, 10,000 feet above the ground. He can attack and kill everyone within 30 feet around me, from 10,000 feet in the air, while he stays in the U.S. Of course, he can because there are times when he can spot where we are. We are not doing anything bad, so of course, we will be like that. I think he is thinking like that. He is thinking that killing both Khamenei and Rouhani will be the end, and that it will make the people start a revolution, a democratic revolution. But I don't think it will be like that. I don't think they will make a move without a leader. I am in the same position as Emperor Showa was. If Emperor Showa were killed, then the 100 million Japanese would have stood up and battled to defend mainland Japan. Just like that, the Americans that come into

Iran will have difficulty fighting fierce guerrillas. El Cantare does not want such an unfortunate future.

"Justice must be judged Based on hard facts"

KHAMENEI'S G.S.

We can still change if they are asking us to change our ways by leading us philosophically, but if they are planning an all-out attack, then we have no choice but to use the porcupine strategy. Our only way is to attack everything that comes near us. I think Israel will be joining the attack. If the U.K. and the U.S. attack, Israel will also attack. On the other hand... This is "Operation Islamic Divide."

FUJII

Yes.

KHAMENEI'S G.S.

I think this is a strategy to prevent Islamic countries from cooperating, so we have to make stronger our Islamic bond. Next, history will be seeing a major world war between Islam and Christianity. The U.S. sees that if Iran develops nuclear weapons, Iran would attack Israel, so they are trying to stop that. That's their real thought. It is, but hmm...

It's not easy to know where justice is in this kind of issue. I don't think people should be the ones to decide. Judgment must be made based on hard facts. We did not attack other nations one-sidedly at all, and for now, we intend to abide by the nuclear agreement, but we are being treated like Iraq.

FUJII

OK. You are saying that Iran is innocent, in front of God, El Cantare...

KHAMENEI'S G.S.

Hmm, but even if Mr. Abe hears it, I don't think he would understand anything.

FUJII

Uh huh.

KHAMENEI'S G.S.

Hmm. Maybe the JSDF will, the Persian Gulf... regarding the oil spill into the Persian Gulf, they will put up oil fences, solidify the oil, and remove it. That is what the JSDF will come to do. I think so. Hmm. But it's not so good.

3

Iran's Claim

Hindering the development of
The most promising country
In the Middle East

FUJII

Thank you for your valuable message today.

KHAMENEI'S G.S.

Japan should also say what it should, and throw the first punch.

FUJII

Uh huh.

KHAMENEI'S G.S.

Uh huh. Yeah. Mr. Trump has experience as a businessperson, but he doesn't know much about world affairs. There are some things he doesn't know about, especially Asia, the Middle East, and the African area. Umm... Ah [*sighs*], Iran is the most promising country in the Middle East. What they are doing is hindering our development, but is it really OK? Of course, we basically think that if Israel grows larger, then that will be a big threat to the Islamic countries in the future. But this is a problem on the Israel side, too. They don't work well with others at all. Really. I hope you will say so.

FUJII

OK. Thank you for your message to Happy Science.

"We will not lose to an ethnic god" "America should set up a global strategy"

KHAMENEI'S G.S.

Umm... OK, if you want to spread El Cantare-belief, you can, but please explain that Islam is a friend religion. Yeah.

FUJII

OK.

KHAMENEI'S G.S.

Hmm. At this rate, I don't think you will make it. I'm very old. People say I'm 79 or 80. I'll be departing to the other world soon. We will not lose to an ethnic god.

FUJII

We have firmly received your message today.

KHAMENEI'S G.S.

At the El Cantare Festival, Master Okawa should say, "Mr. Trump has reached his limits. It's time for him to change his thinking; change 'America First'" and "Now is the time to set up a global strategy."

FUJII

OK. Thank you very much.

KHAMENEI'S G.S.

Uh huh.

Next step should be "Khameneimics" not "Trumponomics"

FUJII

Time is almost up, so is it OK for us to finish here?

KHAMENEI'S G.S.

So that the world will be peaceful. Hmm. [*Holding up* Trumponomics.] You translated this, but it's not enough.

FUJII

Uh huh.

KHAMENEI'S G.S.

It's not good. You have to work harder to introduce Iran's claims more.

FUJII

Yes, we will work hard on it.

KHAMENEI'S G.S.

It's not good. You are cheering for Trump. If you publish this now, it's not good for us. Work hard not to sell this so much. You should make it more expensive.

FUJII

[*Laughs.*]

KHAMENEI'S G.S.

This is 1,800 yen. It's expensive enough, I guess. Hmm, but...

FUJII

We think we have a good understanding of Iran, so please rely on us.

KHAMENEI'S G.S.

You guys worked hard to translate it, so you should sell it for 10,000 yen. Then, you can sell about 1,000 copies within Happy Science. I think that would be good. And, you can study it at your university.

FUJII

Uh huh.

KHAMENEI'S G.S.

Next will be Khamenei... mics? "Khameneimics". Khameneimics. Oil heals everything. Khameneimics. The time will come when Japanese people can use oil freely, as much as they want. This will open the future of Japan. Khameneimics. Yeah.

FUJII

OK, thank you. If we have another opportunity, by all means...

KHAMENEI'S G.S.

Uh huh. Oil for 30 cents per liter, just for Japan. We will sell at the normal price to other countries. Then, Japan will have maglev trains running soon. It takes a lot of energy to run them, you know?

FUJII

Yes. I'm sorry, but it's time for us to end the session. Thank you very much.

KHAMENEI'S G.S.

I'm looking forward [*claps three times*].

FUJII

Thank you for today.

4

Islam Also Needs Reform

RYUHO OKAWA

That was Ayatollah Khamenei. What should I do? It's troublesome.

FUJII

Yes.

RYUHO OKAWA

What shall we do? Hmm... There isn't much reliable information on Iran. I've heard that "more than 10,000 people were arrested," "more than 1,000 people died" or "200 people died."

FUJII

Their Internet has been shut down, so it's difficult to know their situation.

RYUHO OKAWA

It seems like people are being led to believe that Iran is scarier than Xi Jinping or as dangerous as North Korea. It's quite a problem because the American media are all manipulating people in that direction. Countries like Japan can get very little information.

FUJII

Right.

RYUHO OKAWA

However, I believe Islam also needs reform. At this rate, even if the number of their believers increases, we cannot be sure if the world will stabilize. They consider themselves tolerant, but look stubborn to people of other religions and countries. In this point, we have to go back to the time of Muhammad and make some modifications. In terms of economy, it is really troublesome to work with them because they don't believe in interest.

When I used to work for a trading house, I was trading with the Middle East, but I couldn't collect interest because Muhammad denied the concept of interest. However, not being able to collect interest through trade was a trouble for us, so we had to find a way to make up for the interest through other things. So, it was difficult. I think they should get a bit closer to the world standard. It's getting quite serious [*laughs*].

FUJII

Thank you. We wanted to keep the session short today, so we will end it here.

RYUHO OKAWA

If we make it short, they will "attack" me at night, so it doesn't end there [*laughs*].

FUJII

True [*smiles wryly*].

4

Spiritual Interview with The Guardian Spirit of President Trump

Recorded December 14, 2019
Special Lecture Hall, Happy Science, Japan

Donald Trump (1946 - Present)

The 45th president of the United States. Republican. Born in New York City. After graduating from the University of Pennsylvania in 1968, he became known as a real estate magnate, making millions and billions due to his great success in real estate development, and hotel and casino management. Made his presidential announcement in June 2015. With "Make America Great Again" as his slogan, Trump won the hard-fought presidential election in 2016.

Interviewers from Happy Science

Same as Chapter 1.

1

Summoning the Guardian Spirit of Trump to Get His Current Opinion

RYUHO OKAWA

[*To Shio Okawa, who is in the audience.*] Do you have anything else to say? If you do, go ahead.

SHIO OKAWA

Mr. Trump's...

RYUHO OKAWA

Ah. You want to ask what Mr. Trump wants to do? He might change his mind every day, after all.

SHIO OKAWA

Yes.

RYUHO OKAWA

Yesterday, he seemed like he will be making a deal with China, but I'm not sure what he is really thinking.

FUJII

We don't know if that is what he really thinks.

RYUHO OKAWA

He signed the bills regarding human rights and democracy in Hong Kong and regarding human rights in Uyghur, but I'm not sure if there was some secret deal between the U.S. and China or not. And, the U.S. is taking a hard-line stance on North Korea again. Sometimes, he seems like he will attack, but instead negotiate.

FUJII

I guess he is just shaking the opponent.

RYUHO OKAWA

Mr. Trump... [*To Shio Okawa.*] Should we do it? Should we just ask him for his main ideas?

SHIO OKAWA

Yes. I think it's better to record his spiritual messages here than to have me ask him later...

RYUHO OKAWA

Could you ask Mr. Trump just a few important questions?

FUJII

The current trade war, the future of Hong Kong, and Iran. These three.

RYUHO OKAWA

We will just ask what he plans to do.

FUJII

Yes, just his conclusion, in short.

[*Hereafter recorded in English.*]

2

"Xi Jinping is in My Hand"

PRESIDENT TRUMP'S GUARDIAN SPIRIT
Hmm.

FUJII
Hello, Mr. President.

TRUMP'S G.S.
Hmm!

FUJII
I want to ask you just simple questions.

TRUMP'S G.S.
[*Holds up* Trumponomics.] Million seller!

FUJII
Yes, thank you so much.

TRUMP'S G.S.
Million seller!

FUJII
Yes. But now, the Iran issue is very critical.

TRUMP'S G.S.
Hmm.

FUJII
Some kind of decision is going to be made in the world.

TRUMP'S G.S.
Hmm. About what?

FUJII
Beginning a war.

TRUMP'S G.S.
Hmm?

FUJII

War against Iran.

TRUMP'S G.S.

Iran? Yeah!

FUJII

We hope to know your mind.

TRUMP'S G.S.

Oh, I will do my best.

FUJII

And, another issue is the trade war against China.

TRUMP'S G.S.

Ah.

FUJII

You reached an agreement yesterday. What are you going to make of this issue? Are you going to compromise with Xi Jinping China, or not?

TRUMP'S G.S.

Not yet.

FUJII

Not yet?

TRUMP'S G.S.

Not yet.

FUJII

You mean, you haven't decided it yet?

TRUMP'S G.S.

Ah, hmm. I will decide, finally, at the time of solution of Hong Kong problem and Uyghur problem. Yeah. I have the tactics regarding trading matter; up and down, up and down, up and down, and settle. This is the tactics.

FUJII

You mean it's your art of the deal.

TRUMP'S G.S.

Yes. Xi Jinping is in my hand. I can control him. He is very weak now, so he wants to compromise. So, I will lead him to be peaceful, and want to destroy "One Belt, One Road" strategy. I'll make it stop.

3

Asking Top Leader Khamenei To Understand America

FUJII

So, for you, the Iranian problem is not so big an issue, but...

TRUMP'S G.S.

Yeah.

FUJII

...fighting against Xi Jinping is a more important agenda?

TRUMP'S G.S.

Just launch missiles, 100 missiles level. Just alarming them.

YOSHII

About the Middle East, some media reported that thousands of U.S. troops might be sent near Iran, so many people are worrying about the U.S. waging a war against Iran. What is your intention behind the Middle East policy against Iran?

TRUMP'S G.S.

Ah, I want to change their mind. President Rouhani and top leader Khamenei, these two people are against the United States policy, so I want to change their mind, and they should have some kind of, how do I say, understanding regarding the American way of thinking. This is just the battle of the way of thinking.

So, they can change their mind. If Mr. Khamenei comes to America, and at the White House, if he can meet me and have a conversation, and if I can persuade him to stop making nuclear weapons and stop the policy of destroying Israel, if he agreed with me on this point, we can be good friends.

4

Buy American Thinking

FUJII

OK. Thank you so much. Very good information. I think you know well about the mistake in Iraqi War, so we hope you would make a better decision on the Iranian issue.

TRUMP'S G.S.

OK. Please depend on me.

FUJII

Thank you.

TRUMP'S G.S.

I'm cleverer than Mr. Obama, so it's OK. No problem.

FUJII

Yes.

TRUMP'S G.S.

But I'm a good negotiator, so I'll shake their mind and make a great deal. Xi Jinping is just in my hand and dancing in my palm. So, I can deal with them with my free will. Xi Jinping and Khamenei, they are trapped by Donald Trump.

FUJII

OK. Thank you so much. We rely on you.

TRUMP'S G.S.

Yeah. I'm clever because you introduced me to Japanese people.

FUJII

Yes.

TRUMP'S G.S.

Oh, 1 million seller. [*Flipping through* Trumponomics.] 2 million, 10 million seller!

FUJII

Thank you so much.

TRUMP'S G.S.

Japanese people should [*slams* Trumponomics *onto the table*] read this book! It's a final key to solve the world problem. Trumponomics! Not Abenomics!

FUJII

Thank you.

TRUMP'S G.S.

Right?

FUJII

Yes. Good message.

TRUMP'S G.S.

Yeah, you are a good person. You are a light of angel!

FUJII

Yes, thank you. I'll send it to you.

TRUMP'S G.S.

Please, please, please study English, more and more! And, you can introduce me to Japanese people.

FUJII

Many Japanese will understand you through this book. Thank you so much.

TRUMP'S G.S.

Good book. I cannot read Japanese, but it's a good book. Yeah, indeed.

FUJII

It's high time to conclude our conversation. Thank you so much.

TRUMP'S G.S.

Buy, buy, buy, buy America! Buy American... no, American thinking! Yeah.

FUJII

Yes. We hope you would make a good decision. Thank you so much.

TRUMP'S G.S.

Thank you.

5

After the Spiritual Message: Iran Should Make Effort To Be Understood By Others

[Hereafter recorded in Japanese.]

RYUHO OKAWA

He is a negotiator, so we don't know what he will do. I think he will negotiate by praising, criticizing, and shaking. Anyway, we will decide which way to go by talking with God Thoth. Mr. Trump's thinking comes from God Thoth, they think in almost the same way. So, I'll talk to Thoth about this matter. I think Mr. Trump himself is more flexible.

The point was, he wants Ayatollah Khamenei to come to the White House to shake hands and show respect. That was his "final answer". It means he wants to say, "Let's be friends." He is very accepting when it comes to something like this. If the American people can watch on TV, the supreme leader of Iran frankly enjoying his time with the president at the White House and the resort in Florida, they will be convinced. I think that's what Mr. Trump thinks. It might be one way to make Iran a part of the West.

But they seem to be a little stubborn, so the U.S. is planning to put military pressure on them, as much as possible, without going to war. I hope it will not end up like North Korea or like the China-Hong Kong problem. Iran should be a little more flexible.

FUJII
He gave us important messages.

RYUHO OKAWA
They don't have to fight to solve the problem. The other day, Iranian President Rouhani wanted to deliver a speech at the UN, but a U.S. official declined his travel visa. Then, Mr. Trump approved

the visa and said that the U.S. is not so intolerant to reject people who want to visit, and that he is allowed to give a speech. As you can see, Mr. Trump is relatively accepting of people who seek for his help. So, if people are too stubborn and aggressive, they will clash with him.

Ayatollah Khamenei should control his pride a little and visit countries outside of Iran. He should appear in public like how the Japanese emperor goes on his progress. If Iran remains as it is, it will be difficult for Ayatollah Khamenei. Iran should make effort to be understood by others. We published several spiritual messages from Ayatollah Khamenei in Japanese, but even if we dispatch our opinion in Japanese, we cannot reach out to the world.

Ayatollah Khamenei is thinking that if he goes to the U.S., he will be targeted by many groups like the CIA or FBI, I guess. Maybe he watched some American movies and thought that the U.S. is a dangerous place.

FUJII

But in reality, I think the best chance for him is to negotiate with Trump.

RYUHO OKAWA

Mr. Trump usually tries to negotiate with people by creating a crisis, and I think it will be a good idea this time. It will be good for Japan to mediate by going to the U.S. when Iran does. I think it will be good for us to mediate when the Iranian president visits the U.S. for a talk.

I don't recommend going straight into war when its cause is still unclear. It will be quite difficult for Japan because a war would mean one of its oil suppliers will be cut off. Iran does not think so badly of Japan, so we want to be a good bridge for them. And, Russia will also come into play, but we want to work well with them.

(Happiness Realization Party Leader) Ms. Shaku, please do your best. I think the Japanese

Diet will dissolve next year (2020). I don't expect the Japanese mass media to report on HRP, so we hope to let people know through our own efforts that they need HRP.

So, this is what Mr. Trump is thinking. If there is something Happy Science can do to help, we should. But Japanese newspapers and TV stations will not report on us even if we make diplomatic efforts because most of them are non-religious people. So, we cannot count on them to spread our missionary work. They report on the bad things religions do, but not on something like that, so HRP has little power to sell itself.

FUJII
We will do our best.

RYUHO OKAWA
But God's plan might offer us a chance, so we need to be ready for it.

FUJII

Yes. Thank you very much for sharing your precious time with us.

RYUHO OKAWA

Today, we heard very precious opinions as part of information gathering for the El Cantare Festival. Thank you.

FUJII

Thank you.

5

Spiritual Messages from The Guardian Spirit of Prime Minister Abe, The Guardian Spirit of Greta Thunberg, and Gaia

Recorded December 14, 2019
Special Lecture Hall, Happy Science, Japan

Shinzo Abe (1954 - Present)

A Japanese politician (member of the House of Representatives) and the leader of the Liberal Democratic Party. His grandfather, Nobusuke Kishi, was a prime minister, and his father, Shintaro Abe, was a foreign minister. He graduated with a degree in political science from Seikei University. Abe first became a member of the House of Representatives after the election in 1993, and later became the 90th prime minister in Sep. 2006, but resigned after just one year. He was re-elected as the 96th prime minister in Dec. 2012, and again in Dec. 2014 to become the 97th prime minister. Still serving his term as of February 2020.

Greta Thunberg (2003 - Present)

An environmental activist from Stockholm, Sweden. She began the school climate strike in Aug. 2018. It became a worldwide movement, and on Sep. 20, 2019, protests were held in many places across the world, with more than four million young people participating in 163 countries. She gave a speech at the UN Climate Action Summit three days later on Sep. 23.

Gaia

When the core part of El Cantare, Supreme God of the Earth, descended to earth for the first time more than 330 million years ago, He took on the name, "Alpha". Gaia was the wife of Alpha, and is known as Mother Earth in Greek mythology. See Ryuho Okawa, *In Love with the Sun: Spiritual Messages from Goddess Gaia* (Tokyo: Happy Science, 2014). Furthermore, Gaia is now born and living in current Japan as Ryuho Okawa's wife, Shio Okawa.

Interviewer from Happy Science[*]

Shio Okawa
Aide to Master & CEO

No statements made by the guardian spirits of Mr. Shinzo Abe and Ms. Greta Thunberg in this book reflect statements actually made by themselves.

[*] Her professional title represents her position at the time of the interview.

1

The Inner Voice of
Prime Minister Abe's Guardian Spirit

A U.S.-Iran dilemma

SHIO OKAWA

Is anyone there?

PRIME MINISTER ABE'S GUARDIAN SPIRIT

[*Groans several times.*]

SHIO OKAWA

Who are you?

ABE'S G.S.

[*Groans several times.*] Shinzo Abe.

SHIO OKAWA

Good evening.

ABE'S G.S.

Yeah.

SHIO OKAWA

It is half past midnight. What's the problem?

ABE'S G.S.

I don't know what to do with Iran.

SHIO OKAWA

Iran.

ABE'S G.S.

Yeah. They are asking us to mediate, but we cannot at all. We will send the Japan Self-Defense Forces (JSDF), but we can only tell them that we don't intend to attack.

SHIO OKAWA

They have to transport oil.

ABE'S G.S.

No, they are on an oil embargo. They are under sanctions.

SHIO OKAWA

Oh, that's right.

ABE'S G.S.

If Iran's revenue reduces by as much as two-thirds, they cannot survive. It is like the ABCD encirclement of Japan in the past, which means this will lead to war. But even if you ask me, I cannot resolve it.

SHIO OKAWA

Hmm. Master also mentioned that it would be difficult.

ABE'S G.S.

Yes.

SHIO OKAWA

From the standpoint of the prime minister.

ABE'S G.S.

But I cannot stop what the U.S. is trying to do,
either.

SHIO OKAWA

That's true.

ABE'S G.S.

Stock prices rose rapidly because they seem like
they will be shelving the trade war against China.
I cannot but think that they will make their war
against Iran a priority. What can Japan do?

SHIO OKAWA

You are in a dilemma.

ABE'S G.S.

I think Iran's president will just say they didn't do
it. He will say that it is a bias and strategy of the

U.S. I can listen to him and relay it to Mr. Trump, but it will solve nothing.

SHIO OKAWA

Regarding the next election, Mr. Trump is thinking that his people will understand better an attack on Iran more than an attack on China.

ABE'S G.S.

The U.S. has shale oil, shale gas, coal, everything. They can survive without the Middle East. So, they will have no problem. They will not be influenced. Instead, they can create jobs. They will see less and less unemployment every day, but more jobs.

Is "innocent Japan" a fish out of water?

SHIO OKAWA

After all, Prime Minister Abe has an obligation to explain the necessity of nuclear power plants, doesn't he? He is in this predicament because he didn't explain it.

ABE'S G.S.

I can't do it. Looking at the world level, the Pope came to Japan and said, "Stop nuclear power" and now, at the Climate Action Summit...

SHIO OKAWA

"Stop coal"?

ABE'S G.S.

They are telling us to stop coal. How...

SHIO OKAWA

But Ms. Greta will get angry if we don't stop coal, too.

ABE'S G.S.

Hmm. It's getting difficult to import oil from them (Iran) because they are under sanctions. "Innocent Japan" is running dry.

SHIO OKAWA

No, Japan is guilty, too.

ABE'S G.S.

Like a fish out of water.

SHIO OKAWA

Japan is also to blame for trying to be everybody's friend and not thinking about its own defense. Japanese people, I mean. Eventually, they will have to pay for it.

ABE'S G.S.

We don't have enough power to apply sanctions against China, for now.

SHIO OKAWA

I agree with that.

ABE'S G.S.

Chinese customers buy things in Japan, but... I know that more than 80 percent of the Japanese people don't think well of China. Only a little over 10 percent are welcoming, I...

President Trump's reason to attack Iran

SHIO OKAWA

Why, Mr. Trump, Iran...

ABE'S G.S.

For the next election, Mr. Trump wants Jewish votes...

SHIO OKAWA

He approved Judaism as a nationality.

ABE'S G.S.

Jewish people's votes. Many of them are right-wing, so he must get those votes. Without the oil in the Middle East, the U.S. domestic industry such as coal, oil, and gas...

SHIO OKAWA

Ah, those will grow.

ABE'S G.S.

It's better for them in terms of their economy. And, Boris Johnson won, so the joint force of the EU to compete against the U.S. will be weakened a lot. The world will get closer to what Mr. Trump has in mind. He needs to strengthen the U.S. by cooperating with the U.K., while weakening the EU.

SHIO OKAWA

Yes.

ABE'S G.S.

The Germany lady is too left-wing. Really.

SHIO OKAWA

It's the best Mr. Kant* can do.

ABE'S G.S.

It is. You cannot get rid of the gap between the rich
and the poor, no matter how many countries gather
in the EU. And now, Russia is about to save Iran by
lending money. Hmm. The world is heading in a
strange... I think China will say they will buy Iran's
oil. Hmm. It is difficult. Japan will not be able to
buy oil.

---

* According to a spiritual reading by Happy Science, it is believed that
German Chancellor Angela Merkel was born as the philosopher Immanuel
Kant in her past life. See Ryuho Okawa, *Spiritual Interview with the Guardian
Spirit of Angela Merkel: Revealing Her True Intentions, Visions, and Challenges*
(Tokyo: HS Press, 2018).

"I want to spend time Just looking at cherry blossoms"

SHIO OKAWA

Master will investigate the fact and the truth by recording spiritual messages tomorrow, so please use those as a reference.

ABE'S G.S.

Hmm. I want to spend time just looking at cherry blossoms.

SHIO OKAWA

[*Smiles wryly.*] Please don't.

ABE'S G.S.

The Iranian president can come, but I cannot give him a warm reception. There is nothing for me to do.

SHIO OKAWA

But I think the Iranian president is now more depressed than Prime Minister Abe.

ABE'S G.S.

I cannot say, "We will buy oil from you."

SHIO OKAWA

Hmm. Why not? You can.

ABE'S G.S.

Talking about admonition, I have no idea what I should admonish him for. I may be able to tell them to stop being anti-American and not to suppress demonstrations. But those demonstrations occurred because of the inflation resulting from economic sanctions imposed by the U.S. So, I know they will ask us to make the U.S. stop the sanctions.

SHIO OKAWA

But Japan has to become a country which can express its own opinions. The relationship is not equal unless Japan tells its opinions to the U.S.

ABE'S G.S.

I can send JSDF, but it's just a formality. There is no appropriate work for them. Hmm. We don't want to come under drone attacks by guerrillas in the Middle East. It's not like I prefer Iran over Saudi Arabia, or vice versa.

I don't know what to do. We don't have resources nor energy. Our food self-sufficiency is less than 40 percent. Japan is in danger, indeed. And, China is gradually buying up our food.

SHIO OKAWA

But Prime Minister Abe is also to blame for that. He is all the more responsible because he has been in power for a long time.

"I wish people would bash Greta"

ABE'S G.S.

There is nothing more I can do. But I still have the option to restart the nuclear power plants. [*Sighs.*] Umm, I wish people would bash Greta or something, really. I'm in trouble.

SHIO OKAWA

Actually, you would want Greta to say, "Don't use coal and oil" now.

ABE'S G.S.

We will be in trouble.

SHIO OKAWA

We have no choice but to use nuclear power.

ABE'S G.S.

Actually, she is against nuclear power, too. Because the Pope is against it.

SHIO OKAWA

Ah, I guess so. Greta is against nuclear power, also.

ABE'S G.S.

Of course she is. There are only a few other options, such as wind power and solar power.

SHIO OKAWA

Since even the president of Brazil is saying his opinion to Greta, Mr. Abe can give his opinion in Japan. It's OK, I think.

ABE'S G.S.

Hmm. She's like the representative of left-wing people in the world.

"I can do nothing"

SHIO OKAWA

[*About five seconds of silence.*] I heard what you wanted to say, so is it OK?

ABE'S G.S.

I cannot tell the Iranian president not to come. And, there will be nothing I can do, even if he comes. So, can Master Okawa take responsibility and say something at the El Cantare Festival on the 17th (Dec. 2019)?

SHIO OKAWA

But Mr. Abe is the prime minister of a nation, isn't he?

ABE'S G.S.

You know, I can do nothing.

SHIO OKAWA

You can do nothing... If Mr. Abe can do nothing, then Japan can do nothing.

ABE'S G.S.

China is now trying to shelve the Hong Kong problem and shift the focus to the demonstrations in Iran. They are hoping that the U.S. will shift to that matter.

SHIO OKAWA

"Trump, fight against China." We hope so.

ABE'S G.S.

Ah.

SHIO OKAWA

What about Johnson? Is he pro-Chinese or not?

ABE'S G.S.

They are leaving the EU, so their next potential partners are just the U.S., China, and Japan, I guess.

SHIO OKAWA

(The guardian spirit of) Johnson spoke Japanese the other day. OK. Anyway, we will record (spiritual messages) tomorrow.

ABE'S G.S.

I don't understand these kinds of things too well, so please speak on them for me. I hope so.

SHIO OKAWA

Good night.

2

The Raging Guardian Spirit of Greta

"Kick Trump"

SHIO OKAWA

Who are you?

SPIRIT

Umm? [*About 15 seconds of silence.*]

SHIO OKAWA

Who are you? Hmm? Who are you?

SPIRIT

Ah... ah... ah...

SHIO OKAWA

Hmm? You raised your right hand. Go ahead.

SPIRIT

Ah...

SHIO OKAWA

Can you speak Japanese?

SPIRIT

Ah... ah... ah... ah... ah... ah...

SHIO OKAWA

Are you Japanese? Foreigner? English? I guess not.

SPIRIT

Ah... ah... ah... ah...

SHIO OKAWA

EU?

SPIRIT

Ah?

SHIO OKAWA
EU? U.K.?

SPIRIT
Ah... Hah...

SHIO OKAWA
Iran?

SPIRIT
Ah...

SHIO OKAWA
Hong Kong? China? Malaysia? U.S.? Are you an Earthling? Do you know Happy Science?

SPIRIT
Ah, hah.

SHIO OKAWA
Are you a man or a woman?

SPIRIT
Ah... ah...

SHIO OKAWA
Ni hao. Ni hao. Hello. Can you hear me? Who are you?

MS. GRETA'S GUARDIAN SPIRIT
Ah... Ah... Greta.

SHIO OKAWA
Greta? Greta.

GRETA'S G.S.
Greta.

SHIO OKAWA
Thunberg?

GRETA'S G.S.
Thunberg.

SHIO OKAWA

Really? Do you know Happy Science?

GRETA'S G.S.

No.

SHIO OKAWA

Why did you come here?

GRETA'S G.S.

Trump. Kick him.

SHIO OKAWA

(You) Hate him.

GRETA'S G.S.

He is a mother f**ker.

SHIO OKAWA

[*Laughs.*] You did your best to curse in English. I'm sorry, but the gods of some countries are right, I

mean, Putin and Trump. And, Master Okawa who
is above them.

GRETA'S G.S.
Japan... Japan... Japan... Ah...

SHIO OKAWA
Japan is...

GRETA'S G.S.
No brain. No brain.

SHIO OKAWA
How is Japan supposed to live without coal, oil, or
nuclear energy?

GRETA'S G.S.
Eat fish.

SHIO OKAWA
Where do you get the electricity for your
smartphone, Miss Thunberg?

GRETA'S G.S.
Solar panel.

SHIO OKAWA
That requires sunlight. You need global warming to get sunlight, right?

GRETA'S G.S.
No CO_2.

SHIO OKAWA
I'm sorry?

GRETA'S G.S.
No CO_2.

SHIO OKAWA
You are emitting CO_2 just by being alive.

GRETA'S G.S.
Bad country. America, China, Japan. Bad.

SHIO OKAWA

Who told you that?

GRETA'S G.S.

Very bad.

SHIO OKAWA

Who told you that?

GRETA'S G.S.

News.

SHIO OKAWA

News?

GRETA'S G.S.

EU, no. Stop carbon, oil...

SHIO OKAWA

How do you plan to supply enough energy?

GRETA'S G.S.

Wind power, solar panel.

SHIO OKAWA

What about days with no wind?

GRETA'S G.S.

Sleep, sleep.

SHIO OKAWA

So, you are going back to a primitive lifestyle.

GRETA'S G.S.

Might be. Earth, Earth, Earth, the Earth is sinking into deep sea.

SHIO OKAWA

But the Earth itself can think. The Earth is a "Thinkable man." And, it might disagree with you. You might want to study a little bit more, otherwise you could send out the wrong opinion. What Mr.

Trump is saying is correct. You should educate yourself while you are still young. It will keep you from stumbling in the future.

Heavy pressure from the world

GRETA'S G.S.

No more war. Stop Trump.

SHIO OKAWA

Trump is a servant of God, so you can't. Greta is a servant of Lenin*, so she will lose. The clothes you wear are also...

GRETA'S G.S.

Heavy... heavy... heavy... pressure. Heavy, worldwide heavy pressure.

---

* According to a spiritual reading by Happy Science on Sep. 25, 2019, it was revealed that the Soviet leader Vladimir Lenin is spiritually influencing Greta Thunberg. See Ryuho Okawa, *On Carbon footprints reducing: Why Greta gets angry?* (Tokyo: HS Press, 2020).

SHIO OKAWA

Mr. Trump and others are telling you to study about the world a little more. They are being kind to you.

GRETA'S G.S.

Next election in the U.S., my responsibility is to stop Trump from winning the election. Just stop him. He's a crazy man. Stop him. Stop him. Stop him.

SHIO OKAWA

That might be difficult because you do not hold any post in your nation. Please start by reading books of Happy Science.

GRETA'S G.S.

I don't know.

SHIO OKAWA

I'm sorry?

GRETA'S G.S.

I don't know.

SHIO OKAWA

If you don't know, then start by learning.

GRETA'S G.S.

I don't know Happy Science.

SHIO OKAWA

There are many things in this world that you do not know about, so please study. Mr. Trump is right about that. You must not drag many people into your reckless act.

GRETA'S G.S.

Science told us to stop.

SHIO OKAWA

Do you realize that the advancement of the very science you believe in produces a lot of CO_2?

It's not good for you to say, "Believing in science" because we came this far thanks to science. I don't understand what you are trying to say.

Greta believes in Yahweh

GRETA'S G.S.

Very sad about busy people. They will lose their country. Their country is under the sea, almost sinking. I am the Messiah, Messiah of this age. Messiah of this age.

SHIO OKAWA

But you might live 70 more years.

GRETA'S G.S.

I am the Jeanne d'Arc (Joan of Arc), modern Jeanne d'Arc.

SHIO OKAWA

Umm, OK. Do you know Odin?

GRETA'S G.S.

No.

SHIO OKAWA

No? What about Hermes?

GRETA'S G.S.

No.

SHIO OKAWA

Thoth?

GRETA'S G.S.

No.

SHIO OKAWA

Osiris? Loki? Mighty Thor? Zeus? Who is your God?

GRETA'S G.S.
Uh? Yahweh?

SHIO OKAWA
Yahweh? Lenin appeared last time. Do you know Lenin?

GRETA'S G.S.
I don't know.

SHIO OKAWA
See? Like Mr. Trump said, you need to study. If you only spend time doing activities, you will lose sight of yourself because you will get involved with many things.

GRETA'S G.S.
Putin also hates me.

She insists people stop producing CO$_2$,
But does not offer plan B

SHIO OKAWA

How about the Chinese?

GRETA'S G.S.

They are bad CO$_2$-emitting people. But they don't hear Earth.

SHIO OKAWA

Why did you come here, to Master Ryuho Okawa?

GRETA'S G.S.

Stop oil production, coal production, gas production.

SHIO OKAWA

So, how can we, Japanese people, get electricity?

GRETA'S G.S.

I don't know. I don't know.

SHIO OKAWA

"I don't know" means no responsibility. Your words have no responsibility.

GRETA'S G.S.

You have no right to deprive us of our future, children's future.

SHIO OKAWA

But, but, but, you shouldn't use words.

GRETA'S G.S.

Huh?

SHIO OKAWA

You shouldn't use words.

GRETA'S G.S.

Big countries should stop.

SHIO OKAWA

You shouldn't use words you don't have responsibility for.

GRETA'S G.S.

I'm the consciousness of the Earth.

SHIO OKAWA

You?

GRETA'S G.S.

Uh huh.

SHIO OKAWA

I don't think it's true.

GRETA'S G.S.

I am the Gaia.

SHIO OKAWA

I don't think it's true.

GRETA'S G.S.

Gaia is the heart of the Earth. The Earth is running tears.

SHIO OKAWA

Gaia is crying? Then, shall we talk to her?

GRETA'S G.S.

I am the Gaia.

3

The Present and the Future
Seen through the Eyes of Gaia

Greta must learn the true name of God

SHIO OKAWA

Gaia, Gaia. Could you please give a few words to Greta? Gaia, Gaia, the real Gaia.

GAIA

[*About three seconds of silence.*] This is Gaia.

SHIO OKAWA

Greta says she is Gaia.

GAIA

She is wrong.

SHIO OKAWA

What do you think of Earth?

GAIA

Just do as El Cantare says.

SHIO OKAWA

OK.

GAIA

The point is, she must learn the true name of God. It is El Cantare's decision. Rising and falling sea levels, rain, snow, wind, droughts; such kinds of natural disasters are all necessary for Earth's history.

These matters are all up to God. Humans need to repent and correct their mistakes. Greta sees natural disasters as God's punishment and blames adults for it, but she needs to change her way of thinking.

It is meaningless to resist climate change

SHIO OKAWA

Are you crying now?

GAIA

Umm, I'm flying in the sky.

SHIO OKAWA

You're flying. Where exactly?

GAIA

Climate change will occur. It's already been decided, so it's meaningless to resist.

SHIO OKAWA

Then, we don't need to think about it?

GAIA

Climate change is planned, but you have not been told about it. Someone else said this too, but in the beginning, the Earth was magma. The atmosphere was full of CO_2 and sulfur. Earth cooled, and became what it is now. It was not 20 or 30 degrees Celsius as it is now. It was a planet covered in thick gas and at a blazing hundreds of degrees Celsius, just like Venus is now. So, it took a long, long time for life to inhabit Earth. People have forgotten this fact. The Earth has been cooling in its long history. Definitely cooling.

SHIO OKAWA
OK.

GAIA
Right now, the ozone layer is also getting thin. So, although the sunlight reaches Earth's surface, the atmosphere cannot retain its heat. The Sun's energy hits the Earth and heats it up, but this heat is flowing out of the Earth now. Then, there will be intense cooling. There is the ozone hole above Antarctica. This means that the heat is actually...

So, next, there could be not global warming, but global cooling.

If the Earth had atmosphere and the ozone layer was not destroyed, then it would be heated by sunlight, but there is the ozone hole. So, it means that there could be global cooling instead. We don't know which way it will go yet. You shouldn't jump to conclusions.

SHIO OKAWA
OK.

GAIA
Continents can sink and rise. You cannot just think about the rising sea levels due to increase in temperature. The magma is still in motion. The Earth's core is still very hot, at an extremely high temperature of thousands of degrees. This is at the core. If all of this cools off completely, the Earth will become a dead planet. Over the course of the Earth's history, this planet has been cooling for

sure. So, it's not right to only focus on the last 30 years.

SHIO OKAWA
Uh huh.

GAIA
The early Earth, gas... It was covered in CO_2 and sulfur, so nothing could live on it. The ocean was acidic. But now, organisms can live on Earth. Of course, in terms of environmental issue, it is not good to have plastic on the ocean floor or inside fish. But energy issues do not decide everything on this Earth. There was a time when many volcanoes erupted and the Earth was covered in sand and dust. OK? Sometimes there needs to be such a period. It is very difficult for life to be born.

It might be God's plan
For Christianity and Islam to decline

SHIO OKAWA

Is it possible for the desert regions in the Middle East to grow green again?

GAIA

People are researching ways to do that, so it will happen, I think.

SHIO OKAWA

What should Iran do?

GAIA

Hmm. Actually, the Middle East is also to blame. The point is, they do not recognize El Cantare as Allah. It's a difficult problem. We want to protect the Middle East, but spreading their Islamic civilization does not necessarily lead to people's happiness.

We think that the Christian civilization is falling into ruin because of the countless wars and the destruction of families. Islam is also about to perish because they are not keeping up with the times. Both Christianity and Islam think they are expanding, but their level of faith is getting weaker, so it might be God's plan for them to decline. Uh huh. It must be the case.

SHIO OKAWA

I see.

GAIA

I don't think they will admit that El Cantare is the Father of Jesus Christ or the Allah which Muhammad spoke of. Happy Science will have to fight alone, indeed.

The meaning of the Golden Age

GAIA

There will be a world crisis. A crisis always comes when a savior is born. This is what the Golden Age means.

SHIO OKAWA

Are we in a crisis now?

GAIA

Yes, you are.

SHIO OKAWA

Will there be more?

GAIA

Yes. But it also means it's another age of God's descent. The time will come when the world must know this.

The age of Middle Eastern oil
Will end soon

SHIO OKAWA

Then, are there crises already planned?

GAIA

Japan will not prosper in a happy-go-lucky way. It will run into a dead end. Because, if not, it would not change its way.

SHIO OKAWA

OK. I'm sorry.

GAIA

Don't think about protecting the existing religions anymore. Let them take responsibility for this civilization coming to a dead end.

SHIO OKAWA

What about the Iranian people? Mr. Khamenei and Mr. Rouhani?

GAIA

They will pass away. They will. You can do nothing for them, so you cannot save them. Israel is facing a crisis right now. They are trying to incite their enemy. Anyway, you do not need to take responsibility for them. So, it is time to say farewell.

SHIO OKAWA

To Iran?

GAIA

Yes. The age of Middle Eastern oil will end soon.

SHIO OKAWA

OK. What is Mr. Khamenei called in the heavenly world?

GAIA

[*Sighs.*] He will return to the other world soon, so he will be called Khamenei.

SHIO OKAWA

He said he is from the eighth dimension[*].

GAIA

The truth is, people today are trying to overturn the Iranian Revolution, which was about returning to the older times. I think that is fine. Iran must westernize and modernize, or they will not survive. They should end the old regime already. So, you don't need to get so close to them.

SHIO OKAWA

OK.

---

[*] The heavenly world is layered in multiple dimensions. On Earth, there are the ninth dimensional Cosmic Realm, eighth dimensional Tathagata Realm, seventh dimensional Bodhisattva Realm, sixth dimensional Light Realm, fifth dimensional Goodness Realm, fourth dimensional Astral Realm, and third dimensional Earth Realm. The eighth dimension is the world of teachers of humanity, such as religious founders and fathers of philosophy. See aforementioned *The Laws of the Sun*.

"You cannot stop the great shift
In continents and habitat"

GAIA

I'm sorry. You planned this session for the morning, but you had to do it in the middle of the night.

SHIO OKAWA

It's OK. Greta came and said she was Gaia, so I thought I should just call you and...

GAIA

Uh huh. She thinks she is protecting the Earth.

SHIO OKAWA

I see.

GAIA

I'm just saying that you cannot base your decision on the past 30 years only. We know the Earth from the time it was covered in volcanic gas.

SHIO OKAWA

It's a very difficult problem.

GAIA

You cannot stop the great shift in continents and habitat. It's God's will.

SHIO OKAWA

Does that mean Japan will see more crises?

GAIA

Yes.

SHIO OKAWA

OK.

"Let's hope that the new teachings
Will prevail in the world"

GAIA

There will come a time when humanity will not be saved unless you convey the voice of Ryuho Okawa to the world.

SHIO OKAWA
Right.

GAIA

Enough with Christianity and Islam. Enough with misguided Small Vehicle Buddhism. Enough with Japanese Shintoism, which is empty. It is a waste of time to care about them. Let's hope that the new teachings will prevail in the world. We must spread this all over the world within the next 20 years or so.

SHIO OKAWA

Yes.

GAIA

So, Christianity, Islam...

SHIO OKAWA

We don't need to support Christianity and Islam anymore?

GAIA

No. It will be meaningless. They will fight. Islam will, and Judaism in Israel will, too. You don't need to get involved in their battle. They are already finished. A new religion has already appeared to save people. There will be misfortune on Earth unless they admit that a religion greater than theirs has appeared.

SHIO OKAWA

I understand.

GAIA

OK. Greta is not Gaia. She might believe she is the mother of Earth, but it's not true at all, just her imagination.

SHIO OKAWA

I see. Thank you.

GAIA

Uh huh.

Afterword

We recorded the Chapter 5 Q&A session at midnight, before recording the contents of Chapters 1 to 4.

Japanese Prime Minister Abe was worried about Iranian President Rouhani coming to Japan, because there's nothing he could do. Also, we recorded the anger of Greta's guardian spirit, which Japan could not deal with and became the reason why Japanese Minister of the Environment Koizumi received the Fossil of the Day award during the Climate Action Summit. The 16-year-old girl even claimed herself to be Gaia, who is sometimes called the Life of Earth.

So, we called the real Gaia, who is actually in the Real World, and confirmed the truth.

If Japan fails to take appropriate measures against Greta Thunberg, it will be at risk of falling into becoming a developing country.

Do not allow this ignorant hysterical girl to be the savior of Earth. Be very cautious. Devil-like beings are controlling her from behind.

Ryuho Okawa
Master & CEO of Happy Science Group
Dec. 23, 2019

ABOUT THE AUTHOR

Founder and CEO of Happy Science Group.

Ryuho Okawa was born on July 7th 1956, in Tokushima, Japan. After graduating from the University of Tokyo with a law degree, he joined a Tokyo-based trading house. While working at its New York headquarters, he studied international finance at the Graduate Center of the City University of New York. In 1981, he attained Great Enlightenment and became aware that he is El Cantare with a mission to bring salvation to all humankind.

In 1986, he established Happy Science. It now has members in over 165 countries across the world, with more than 700 branches and temples as well as 10,000 missionary houses around the world.

He has given over 3,400 lectures (of which more than 150 are in English) and published over 3,000 books (of which more than 600 are Spiritual Interview Series), and many are translated into 40 languages. Along with *The Laws of the Sun* and *The Laws Of Messiah*, many of the books have become best sellers or million sellers. To date, Happy Science has produced 25 movies. The original story and original concept were given by the Executive Producer Ryuho Okawa. He has also composed music and written lyrics of over 450 pieces.

Moreover, he is the Founder of Happy Science University and Happy Science Academy (Junior and Senior High School), Founder and President of the Happiness Realization Party, Founder and Honorary Headmaster of Happy Science Institute of Government and Management, Founder of IRH Press Co., Ltd., and the Chairperson of NEW STAR PRODUCTION Co., Ltd. and ARI Production Co., Ltd.

WHAT IS EL CANTARE?

El Cantare means "the Light of the Earth," and is the Supreme God of the Earth who has been guiding humankind since the beginning of Genesis. He is whom Jesus called Father and Muhammad called Allah, and is *Ame-no-Mioya-Gami*, Japanese Father God. Different parts of El Cantare's core consciousness have descended to Earth in the past, once as Alpha and another as Elohim. His branch spirits, such as Shakyamuni Buddha and Hermes, have descended to Earth many times and helped to flourish many civilizations. To unite various religions and to integrate various fields of study in order to build a new civilization on Earth, a part of the core consciousness has descended to Earth as Master Ryuho Okawa.

Alpha is a part of the core consciousness of El Cantare who descended to Earth around 330 million years ago. Alpha preached Earth's Truths to harmonize and unify Earth-born humans and space people who came from other planets.

Elohim is a part of El Cantare's core consciousness who descended to Earth around 150 million years ago. He gave wisdom, mainly on the differences of light and darkness, good and evil.

Ame-no-Mioya-Gami (Japanese Father God) is the Creator God and the Father God who appears in the ancient literature, *Hotsuma Tsutae*. It is believed that He descended on the foothills of Mt. Fuji about 30,000 years ago and built the Fuji dynasty, which is the root of the Japanese civilization. With justice as the central pillar, Ame-no-Mioya-Gami's teachings spread to ancient civilizations of other countries in the world.

Shakyamuni Buddha was born as a prince into the Shakya Clan in India around 2,600 years ago. When he was 29 years old, he renounced the world and sought enlightenment. He later attained Great Enlightenment and founded Buddhism.

Hermes is one of the 12 Olympian gods in Greek mythology, but the spiritual Truth is that he taught the teachings of love and progress around 4,300 years ago that became the origin of the current Western civilization. He is a hero that truly existed.

Ophealis was born in Greece around 6,500 years ago and was the leader who took an expedition to as far as Egypt. He is the God of miracles, prosperity, and arts, and is known as Osiris in the Egyptian mythology.

Rient Arl Croud was born as a king of the ancient Incan Empire around 7,000 years ago and taught about the mysteries of the mind. In the heavenly world, he is responsible for the interactions that take place between various planets.

Thoth was an almighty leader who built the golden age of the Atlantic civilization around 12,000 years ago. In the Egyptian mythology, he is known as god Thoth.

Ra Mu was a leader who built the golden age of the civilization of Mu around 17,000 years ago. As a religious leader and a politician, he ruled by uniting religion and politics.

WHAT IS A SPIRITUAL MESSAGE?

We are all spiritual beings living on this earth. The following is the mechanism behind Master Ryuho Okawa's spiritual messages.

1 You are a spirit

People are born into this world to gain wisdom through various experiences and return to the other world when their lives end. We are all spirits and repeat this cycle in order to refine our souls.

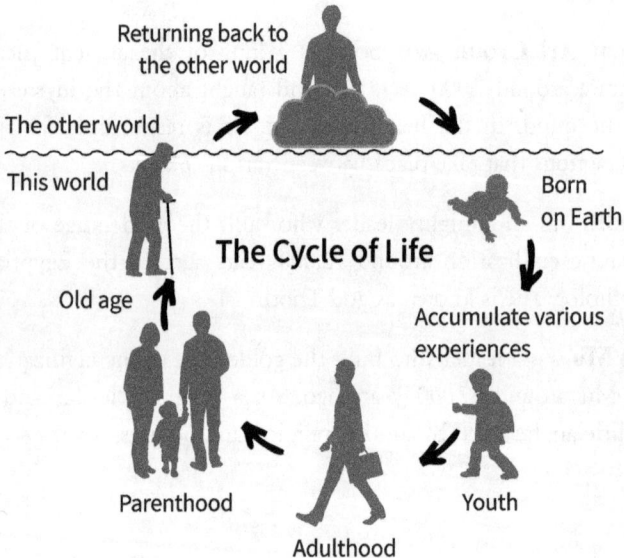

Returning back to the other world

The other world

This world

Born on Earth

The Cycle of Life

Old age

Accumulate various experiences

Parenthood

Adulthood

Youth

2 You have a guardian spirit

Guardian spirits are those who protect the people who are living on this earth. Each of us has a guardian spirit that watches over us and guides us from the other world. They were us in our past life, and are identical in how we think.

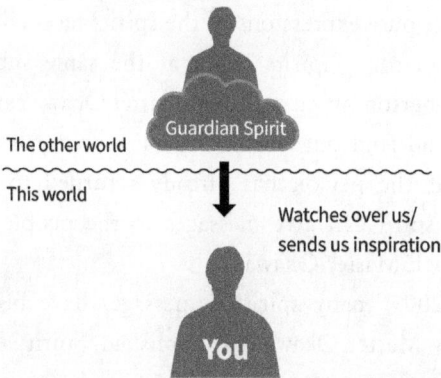

The other world

This world

Watches over us/
sends us inspiration

You

3 How spiritual messages work

Master Ryuho Okawa, through his enlightenment, is capable of summoning any spirit from anywhere in the world, including the spirit world.

Master Okawa's way of receiving spiritual messages is fundamentally different from that of other psychic mediums who undergo trances and are thereby completely taken over by the spirits they are channeling.

Master Okawa's attainment of a high level of enlightenment enables him to retain full control of his consciousness and body throughout the duration of the spiritual message. To allow the spirits to express their own thoughts and personalities freely, however, Master Okawa usually softens the dominancy of his consciousness. This way, he is able to keep his own philosophies out of the way and ensure that the spiritual messages are pure expressions of the spirits he is channeling.

Since guardian spirits think at the same subconscious level as the person living on earth, Master Okawa can summon the spirit and find out what the person on earth is actually thinking. If the person has already returned to the other world, the spirit can give messages to the people living on earth through Master Okawa.

Since 2009, many spiritual messages have been openly recorded by Master Okawa and published. Spiritual messages from the guardian spirits of people living today such as Donald Trump, former Japanese Prime Minister Shinzo Abe and Chinese President Xi Jinping, as well as spiritual messages sent from the spirit world by Jesus Christ, Muhammad, Thomas Edison, Mother Teresa, Steve Jobs and Nelson Mandela are just a tiny pack of spiritual messages that were published so far.

Domestically, in Japan, these spiritual messages are being read by a wide range of politicians and mass media, and the high-level contents of these books are delivering an impact even more on politics, news and public opinion. In recent years, there have been spiritual messages recorded in English, and English translations are being done on the spiritual messages given in Japanese. These have been published overseas, one after another, and have started to shake the world.

1 The guardian spirit / spirit in the other world…

2 Goes inside Master Okawa in this world

3 Master Okawa speaks the words of the guardian spirit / spirit

For more about spiritual messages and a complete list of books in the Spiritual Interview Series, visit okawabooks.com

ABOUT HAPPY SCIENCE

Happy Science is a global movement that empowers individuals to find purpose and spiritual happiness and to share that happiness with their families, societies, and the world. With more than 12 million members around the world, Happy Science aims to increase awareness of spiritual truths and expand our capacity for love, compassion, and joy so that together we can create the kind of world we all wish to live in.

Activities at Happy Science are based on the Principle of Happiness (Love, Wisdom, Self-Reflection, and Progress). This principle embraces worldwide philosophies and beliefs, transcending boundaries of culture and religions.

Love teaches us to give ourselves freely without expecting anything in return; it encompasses giving, nurturing, and forgiving.

Wisdom leads us to the insights of spiritual truths, and opens us to the true meaning of life and the will of God (the universe, the highest power, Buddha).

Self-Reflection brings a mindful, nonjudgmental lens to our thoughts and actions to help us find our truest selves—the essence of our souls—and deepen our connection to the highest power. It helps us attain a clean and peaceful mind and leads us to the right life path.

Progress emphasizes the positive, dynamic aspects of our spiritual growth—actions we can take to manifest and spread happiness around the world. It's a path that not only expands our soul growth, but also furthers the collective potential of the world we live in.

PROGRAMS AND EVENTS

The doors of Happy Science are open to all. We offer a variety of programs and events, including self-exploration and self-growth programs, spiritual seminars, meditation and contemplation sessions, study groups, and book events.

Our programs are designed to:
* Deepen your understanding of your purpose and meaning in life
* Improve your relationships and increase your capacity to love unconditionally
* Attain peace of mind, decrease anxiety and stress, and feel positive
* Gain deeper insights and a broader perspective on the world
* Learn how to overcome life's challenges
  ... and much more.

For more information, visit <u>happy-science.org</u>.

OUR ACTIVITIES

Happy Science does other various activities to provide support for those in need.

♦ **You Are An Angel! General Incorporated Association**

Happy Science has a volunteer network in Japan that encourages and supports children with disabilities as well as their parents and guardians.

♦ **Never Mind School for Truancy**

At 'Never Mind,' we support students who find it very challenging to attend schools in Japan. We also nurture their self-help spirit and power to rebound against obstacles in life based on Master Okawa's teachings and faith.

♦ **"Prevention Against Suicide" Campaign since 2003**

A nationwide campaign to reduce suicides; over 20,000 people commit suicide every year in Japan. "The Suicide Prevention Website-Words of Truth for You-" presents spiritual prescriptions for worries such as depression, lost love, extramarital affairs, bullying and work-related problems, thereby saving many lives.

♦ **Support for Anti-bullying Campaigns**

Happy Science provides support for a group of parents and guardians, Network to Protect Children from Bullying, a general incorporated foundation launched in Japan to end bullying, including those that can even be called a criminal offense. So far, the network received more than 5,000 cases and resolved 90% of them.

- **The Golden Age Scholarship**

  This scholarship is granted to students who can contribute greatly and bring a hopeful future to the world.

- **Success No.1**
  Buddha's Truth Afterschool Academy

  Happy Science has over 180 classrooms throughout Japan and in several cities around the world that focus on afterschool education for children. The education focuses on faith and morals in addition to supporting children's school studies.

- **Angel Plan V**

  For children under the age of kindergarten, Happy Science holds classes for nurturing healthy, positive, and creative boys and girls.

- **Future Stars Training Department**

  The Future Stars Training Department was founded within the Happy Science Media Division with the goal of nurturing talented individuals to become successful in the performing arts and entertainment industry.

- **NEW STAR PRODUCTION Co., Ltd.**
  ARI Production Co., Ltd.

  We have companies to nurture actors and actresses, artists, and vocalists. They are also involved in film production.

CONTACT INFORMATION

Happy Science is a worldwide organization with branches and temples around the globe. For a comprehensive list, visit the worldwide directory at *happy-science.org*. The following are some of the many Happy Science locations:

UNITED STATES AND CANADA

New York
79 Franklin St., New York, NY 10013, USA
Phone: 1-212-343-7972
Fax: 1-212-343-7973
Email: ny@happy-science.org
Website: happyscience-usa.org

New Jersey
66 Hudson St., #2R, Hoboken, NJ 07030, USA
Phone: 1-201-313-0127
Email: nj@happy-science.org
Website: happyscience-usa.org

Chicago
2300 Barrington Rd., Suite #400,
Hoffman Estates, IL 60169, USA
Phone: 1-630-937-3077
Email: chicago@happy-science.org
Website: happyscience-usa.org

Florida
5208 8th St., Zephyrhills, FL 33542, USA
Phone: 1-813-715-0000
Fax: 1-813-715-0010
Email: florida@happy-science.org
Website: happyscience-usa.org

Atlanta
1874 Piedmont Ave., NE Suite 360-C
Atlanta, GA 30324, USA
Phone: 1-404-892-7770
Email: atlanta@happy-science.org
Website: happyscience-usa.org

San Francisco
525 Clinton St.
Redwood City, CA 94062, USA
Phone & Fax: 1-650-363-2777
Email: sf@happy-science.org
Website: happyscience-usa.org

Los Angeles
1590 E. Del Mar Blvd., Pasadena, CA 91106, USA
Phone: 1-626-395-7775
Fax: 1-626-395-7776
Email: la@happy-science.org
Website: happyscience-usa.org

Orange County
16541 Gothard St. Suite 104
Huntington Beach, CA 92647
Phone: 1-714-659-1501
Email: oc@happy-science.org
Website: happyscience-usa.org

San Diego
7841 Balboa Ave. Suite #202
San Diego, CA 92111, USA
Phone: 1-626-395-7775
Fax: 1-626-395-7776
E-mail: sandiego@happy-science.org
Website: happyscience-usa.org

Hawaii
Phone: 1-808-591-9772
Fax: 1-808-591-9776
Email: hi@happy-science.org
Website: happyscience-usa.org

Kauai
3343 Kanakolu Street, Suite 5
Lihue, HI 96766, USA
Phone: 1-808-822-7007
Fax: 1-808-822-6007
Email: kauai-hi@happy-science.org
Website: happyscience-usa.org

Toronto
845 The Queensway
Etobicoke, ON M8Z 1N6, Canada
Phone: 1-416-901-3747
Email: toronto@happy-science.org
Website: happy-science.ca

Vancouver
#201-2607 East 49th Avenue,
Vancouver, BC, V5S 1J9, Canada
Phone: 1-604-437-7735
Fax: 1-604-437-7764
Email: vancouver@happy-science.org
Website: happy-science.ca

INTERNATIONAL

Tokyo
1-6-7 Togoshi, Shinagawa,
Tokyo, 142-0041, Japan
Phone: 81-3-6384-5770
Fax: 81-3-6384-5776
Email: tokyo@happy-science.org
Website: happy-science.org

Seoul
74, Sadang-ro 27-gil,
Dongjak-gu, Seoul, Korea
Phone: 82-2-3478-8777
Fax: 82-2-3478-9777
Email: korea@happy-science.org
Website: happyscience-korea.org

London
3 Margaret St.
London, W1W 8RE United Kingdom
Phone: 44-20-7323-9255
Fax: 44-20-7323-9344
Email: eu@happy-science.org
Website: www.happyscience-uk.org

Taipei
No. 89, Lane 155, Dunhua N. Road,
Songshan District, Taipei City 105, Taiwan
Phone: 886-2-2719-9377
Fax: 886-2-2719-5570
Email: taiwan@happy-science.org
Website: happyscience-tw.org

Sydney
516 Pacific Highway, Lane Cove North,
2066 NSW, Australia
Phone: 61-2-9411-2877
Fax: 61-2-9411-2822
Email: sydney@happy-science.org

Kuala Lumpur
No 22A, Block 2, Jalil Link Jalan Jalil
Jaya 2, Bukit Jalil 57000,
Kuala Lumpur, Malaysia
Phone: 60-3-8998-7877
Fax: 60-3-8998-7977
Email: malaysia@happy-science.org
Website: happyscience.org.my

Sao Paulo
Rua. Domingos de Morais 1154,
Vila Mariana, Sao Paulo SP
CEP 04010-100, Brazil
Phone: 55-11-5088-3800
Email: sp@happy-science.org
Website: happyscience.com.br

Kathmandu
Kathmandu Metropolitan City,
Ward No. 15, Ring Road, Kimdol,
Sitapaila Kathmandu, Nepal
Phone: 977-1-427-2931
Email: nepal@happy-science.org

Jundiai
Rua Congo, 447, Jd. Bonfiglioli
Jundiai-CEP, 13207-340, Brazil
Phone: 55-11-4587-5952
Email: jundiai@happy-science.org

Kampala
Plot 877 Rubaga Road, Kampala
P.O. Box 34130 Kampala, UGANDA
Phone: 256-79-4682-121
Email: uganda@happy-science.org

ABOUT HAPPINESS REALIZATION PARTY

The Happiness Realization Party (HRP) was founded in May 2009 by Master Ryuho Okawa as part of the Happy Science Group. HRP strives to improve the Japanese society, based on three basic political principles of "freedom, democracy, and faith," and let Japan promote individual and public happiness from Asia to the world as a leader nation.

1) Diplomacy and Security: Protecting Freedom, Democracy, and Faith of Japan and the World from China's Totalitarianism

Japan's current defense system is insufficient against China's expanding hegemony and the threat of North Korea's nuclear missiles. Japan, as the leader of Asia, must strengthen its defense power and promote strategic diplomacy together with the nations which share the values of freedom, democracy, and faith. Further, HRP aims to realize world peace under the leadership of Japan, the nation with the spirit of religious tolerance.

2) Economy: Early economic recovery through utilizing the "wisdom of the private sector"

Economy has been damaged severely by the novel coronavirus originated in China. Many companies have been forced into bankruptcy or out of business. What is needed for economic recovery now is not subsidies and regulations by the government, but policies which can utilize the "wisdom of the private sector."

For more information, visit en.hr-party.jp

ABOUT HS PRESS

HS Press is an imprint of IRH Press Co., Ltd. IRH Press Co., Ltd., based in Tokyo, was founded in 1987 as a publishing division of Happy Science. IRH Press publishes religious and spiritual books, journals, magazines and also operates broadcast and film production enterprises. For more information, visit *okawabooks.com*.

Follow us on:

f Facebook: Okawa Books   ⓘ Instagram: OkawaBooks

▶ Youtube: Okawa Books   🐦 Twitter: Okawa Books

𝓟 Pinterest: Okawa Books   g Goodreads: Ryuho Okawa

--------- **NEWSLETTER** ---------

To receive book related news, promotions and events, please subscribe to our newsletter below.

🔗 eepurl.com/bsMeJj

--------- **AUDIO / VISUAL MEDIA** ---------

YOUTUBE

PODCAST

Introduction of Ryuho Okawa's titles; topics ranging from self-help, current affairs, spirituality, religion, and the universe.

BOOKS BY RYUHO OKAWA

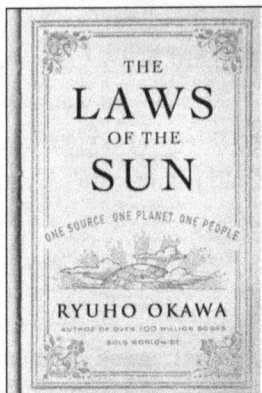

THE LAWS OF THE SUN
ONE SOURCE, ONE PLANET, ONE PEOPLE

Paperback • 288 pages • $15.95
ISBN: 978-1-942125-43-3

IMAGINE IF YOU COULD ASK GOD why He created this world and what spiritual laws He used to shape us—and everything around us. If we could understand His designs and intentions, we could discover what our goals in life should be and whether our actions move us closer to those goals or farther away.

At a young age, a spiritual calling prompted Ryuho Okawa to outline what he innately understood to be universal truths for all humankind. In *The Laws of the Sun*, Okawa outlines these laws of the universe and provides a road map for living one's life with greater purpose and meaning.

In this powerful book, Ryuho Okawa reveals the transcendent nature of consciousness and the secrets of our multidimensional universe and our place in it. By understanding the different stages of love and following the Buddhist Eightfold Path, he believes we can speed up our eternal process of development. *The Laws of the Sun* shows the way to realize true happiness—a happiness that continues from this world through the other.

For a complete list of books, visit **okawabooks.com**

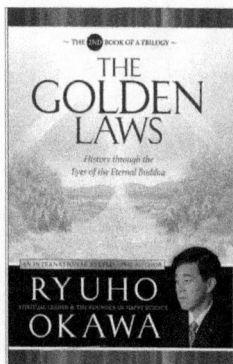

THE GOLDEN LAWS
HISTORY THROUGH THE EYES OF THE ETERNAL BUDDHA

Paperback • 201 pages • $14.95
ISBN: 978-1-941779-81-1

Throughout history, Great Guiding Spirits of Light have been present on Earth in both the East and the West at crucial points in human history to further our spiritual development. *The Golden Laws* reveals how Divine Plan has been unfolding on Earth, and outlines 5,000 years of the secret history of humankind. Once we understand the true course of history, through past, present and into the future, we cannot help but become aware of the significance of our spiritual mission in the present age.

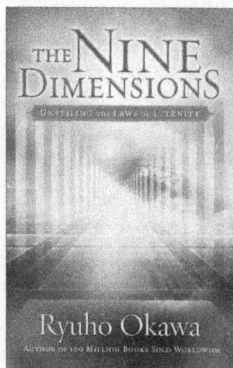

THE NINE DIMENSIONS
UNVEILING THE LAWS OF ETERNITY

Paperback • 168 pages • $15.95
ISBN: 978-0-982698-56-3

This book is a window into the mind of our loving God, who designed this world and the vast, wondrous world of our afterlife as a school with many levels through which our souls learn and grow. When the religions and cultures of the world discover the truth of their common spiritual origin, they will be inspired to accept their differences, come together under faith in God, and build an era of harmony and peaceful progress on Earth.

For a complete list of books, visit **okawabooks.com**

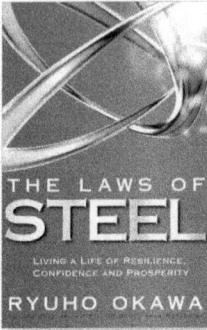

THE LAWS OF STEEL

LIVING A LIFE OF RESILIENCE,
CONFIDENCE AND PROSPERITY

Paperback • 264 pages • $16.95
ISBN: 978-1-942125-65-5

This book is a compilation of six lectures that Ryuho Okawa gave in 2018 and 2019, each containing passionate messages for us to open a brighter future. This powerful and inspiring book will not only show us the ways to achieve true happiness and prosperity, but also the ways to solve many global issues we now face.

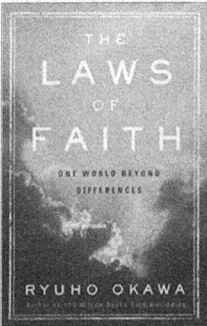

THE LAWS OF FAITH

ONE WORLD BEYOND DIFFERENCES

Paperback • 208 pages • $15.95
ISBN: 978-1-942125-34-1

Ryuho Okawa preaches at the core of a new universal religion from various angles while integrating logical and spiritual viewpoints in mind with current world situations. This book offers us the key to accept diversities beyond differences to create a world filled with peace and prosperity.

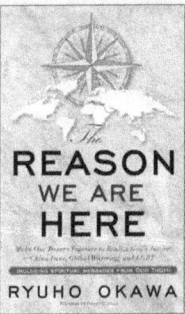

THE REASON WE ARE HERE

MAKE OUR POWERS TOGETHER TO REALIZE
GOD'S JUSTICE -CHINA ISSUE, GLOBAL
WARMING, AND LGBT-

Paperback • 215 pages • $14.95
ISBN: 978-1-943869-62-6

The Reason We Are Here is a book of thought that is unlike any other: its global perspective, timely opinion on current issues, and spiritual class are unmatched. The main content is the lecture in Toronto, Canada given in October 2019 by Ryuho Okawa, a Japanese spiritual leader and the national teacher of Japan.

For a complete list of books, visit **okawabooks.com**

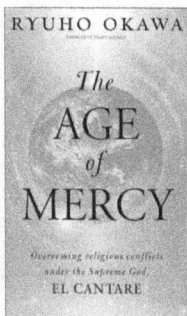

The Age of Mercy
Overcoming religious conflicts under the Supreme God, El Cantare

Hardcover • 110 pages • $22.95
ISBN: 978-1-943869-51-0

Why are there conflicts in the world? How can people understand each other better? This book is a message from the Supreme God who has been guiding humankind from the beginning of creation.

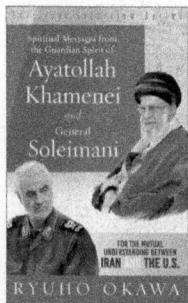

Spiritual Messages from the Guardian Spirit of Ayatollah Khamenei and General Soleimani
For the Mutual Understanding between Iran and the U.S.

Paperback • 165 pages • $11.95
ISBN: 978-1-943869-63-3

In January 2020, Soleimani was killed in Iraq. Only a day after the drone attack, his spirit visited Okawa in Tokyo. Chapter 1 is a record of the spiritual session. Chapter 2 is the record of the spiritual session with the guardian spirit of Ayatollah Khamenei who visited three days later.

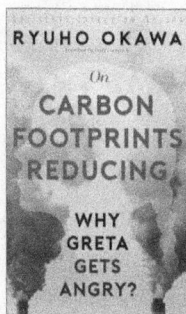

On Carbon Footprints Reducing
Why Greta gets angry?

Paperback • 135 pages • $11.95
ISBN: 978-1-943869-59-6

Greta Thunberg, a 16-year-old environmental activist from Sweden, gave a speech at the United Nations Climate Actions Summit that shocked the world in September 2019. In this book, Okawa summons the spiritual beings who have influence on Greta, and has them speak their true intention as to why they made her say what she said.

---

*For a complete list of books, visit **okawabooks.com***

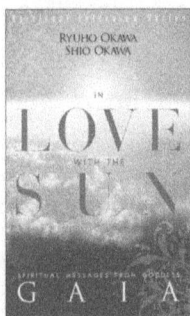

In Love with the Sun

Spiritual Messages from Goddess Gaia

Paperback • 119 pages • $14.95
ISBN: 978-1-941779-26-2

After 600 million years, people shall know the true genesis. The true story when the Earth was born, the guiding concept of the Earth, the mechanism of creating life on Earth. And the future that human beings has to seek, these secrets are now revealed by the spiritual message from Goddess Gaia, who supported the creation of Earth civilization by Alpha, the God of origin.

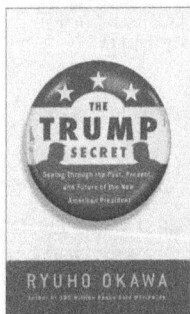

The Trump Secret

Seeing Through the Past, Present, and Future of the New American President

Paperback • 208 pages • $14.95
ISBN: 978-1-942125-22-8

This book contains a series of lectures and interviews that unveil the secrets to Trump's victory and makes predictions of what will happen under his presidency. This book predicts the coming of a new America that will go through a great transformation from the "red and blue states" to the United States.

Spiritual Interview with the Guardian Spirit of Angela Merkel

Revealing Her True Intentions, Visions, and Challenges

Paperback • 105 pages • $9.95
ISBN: 978-1-943869-45-9

In this book, Merkel's subconscious speaks on the concept of the EU using extremely theoretical and philosophical words. Read on and you will see why in the latter half of the interview. Chancellor Merkel is the reincarnation of a great German philosopher who had a profound impact on the founding concept of the League of Nations.

*For a complete list of books, visit **okawabooks.com***

For a complete list of books, visit **okawabooks.com**

MUSIC BY RYUHO OKAWA

El Cantare Ryuho Okawa Original Songs

A song celebrating Lord God

A song celebrating Lord God,
the God of the Earth,
who is beyond a prophet.

DVD
CD

The Water Revolution
English and Chinese version

For the truth and happiness of
the 1.4 billion people in China
who have no freedom. Love,
justice, and sacred rage of God
are on this melody that will
give you courage to fight to
bring peace.

DVD

CD

Search on YouTube

the water revolution 🔍 for a short ad!

Listen now today!

Download from
🎧 **Spotify iTunes Amazon**

DVD, CD available at amazon.com,
and Happy Science locations worldwide

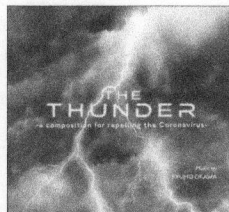